1989 Edition

TOUR de FRANCE

Phil Liggett

TOUR de FRANCE

Phil Liggett

Published in association with
Channel Four Television Company
and The *Daily Telegraph*

A CHANNEL FOUR BOOK

The Daily Telegraph

HARRAP

London

DAVID SAUNDERS
A friend of journalists
and cyclists alike,
to whose memory this
book is dedicated.

PHIL LIGGETT
London, May 1989

First published in Great Britain 1989
by HARRAP BOOKS LIMITED
19–23 Ludgate Hill, London EC4M 7PD
in association with Channel Four
Television Company and
The Daily Telegraph

© Phil Liggett 1989

ISBN 0 245-54826-2

Designed by Schermuly Design Co.

Printed and bound in Italy
by arrangement with Graphicom, Vicenza

The author and publishers would like to thank
the following for permission to reproduce
copyright photographs in this book:

Leo Mason: *page* 99

Phil O'Connor: *pages* 30 (right), 32, 110 (above),
123

Photosport International: *pages* 5, 15, 19, 23
(left), 26, 29, 38, 39, 40, 41, 47, 49, 53, 54
(below), 65, 66, 67, 71, 73, 74, 75, 78, 82, 83, 88,
91, 108, 111 (left), 117, 125 (left), 127, 129, 130,
132, 133, 134, 135, 138, 139, 141, 145, 146
(below), 149, 150, 151

John A. Pierce: *page* 144

Presse-Sport (from John Hillelson): *pages* 11, 13,
14, 15, 16, 20, 23 (right: above *and* below), 24,
50, 54 (above), 59, 62, 69, 76, 79, 87, 104, 120,
121, 131, 136

Sports Pictures (UK) Ltd: *pages* 27, 34, 85, 96,
119, 136

Graham Watson: Front end paper, title page,
pages 30 (left), 37 (left *and* above), 45, 57, 58,
60, 81, 101, 102, 103, 110 (below), 111 (above),
112, 113, 114, 115, 122, 125 (above), 126, 146
(above)

Illustration on page 124 by **Mike Smart**

Contents

Foreword

The Tour de France is THE race for a cyclist, and even if a rider wins a single-day classic race, if he doesn't do a good ride in the Tour his career has not been completed. Only nine riders from each team are accepted in the race, and most top teams have at least sixteen — they would all give an arm and a leg to be in the race. They want to ride for glory, and to say they've made Paris. Why do they keep on going when they have injuries? It's because you never say 'stop' in the Tour, and you either arrive in a box or on your bike in Paris.

You initially aim to finish each day, and you do not think any further, but when you arrive on the Champs-Élysées you say, 'This is Paris, the greatest Avenue in the world, and you've made it!' When I won the Tour in Paris it was all too emotional to appreciate the achievement, but in my other Tours there were tears in my eyes on the Champs-Élysées.

To get there each time, I've gone to Hell and back; argued with my team-mates, punctured, suffered from crashes, but got there! When you arrive you just slump over the handlebars and try to compose yourself before the Press arrive.

The Tour is a commercial operation, and it's so big. For a rider it's like being born again to take part. But when you are selected for the Tour you must remember that you are a professional, and it's also your job to do well. In recent years the race has become even harder. Everyone wants to win it, as they get so much publicity, and they seem to race all of the time now.

My greatest memory, perhaps, is when I shook hands with Pedro Delgado after the crucial time-trial in Dijon which decided the 1987 race in my favour. We each said, 'Well done.' It was a big moment for both of us; I'd won the Tour and he'd lost it, but we both appreciated each other's efforts.

I was delighted that Pedro won the race last year, and without taking anything from his achievement, the rest of the field were no match for him. But I've beaten him before, so maybe it's possible to do it again.

I have been injured, and until the Tour starts I won't know if I can do it again. I hope so.

Stephen Roche
Dublin, 1989

Chapter 1
How it started

Did Pedro Delgado win the 1988 Tour de France, or was he doped? Should he ever have been declared positive as a result of an automatic test for winning a stage when the product he was accused of taking was not on the banned list of substances in cycling? It is a debate that will have no ending; the medical experts have mixed opinions, and so do the riders. One thing is certain: if Pedro Delgado takes the same substance in 1989 he will be penalized, as the cycling list has since been modified. In a few years' time this tale will be just another colourful addition to the long history of the Tour de France.

Since the first Tour took place in 1903, the *Grande Boucle* (the 'Big Loop' — referring to the shape of the route) has been held almost every year, the only stoppage having been caused by the two World Wars.

An account of the colourful history of the race could easily fill three volumes. The founder, Henri Desgrange, shocked Tour followers when he was obliged to arrive at a stage finish on horseback after his car had broken down, but he was already showing the Tour spirit that prevails among the riders even today — you never give up unless you are carried away.

The Tour has faced just about every known problem: strikes by both riders and onlookers; doping scandals; corruption among riders (disqualifications in the early years almost made Desgrange give up the Tour); and terrorist action. No one disputes that this annual race is the most severe of all sporting endurance tests, and what makes its four thousand kilometres even harder is that the selected riders also cover another forty thousand kilometres riding and training during the cycling season. Since 1903, fewer than ten thousand riders have competed in the Tour de France. Of these just over half have finished. In any one season in Europe and the Americas there are perhaps a thousand professionals, of whom only two hundred will find a place in the Tour. Out of these two hundred, only ten at the most will be seen to have the ability to win.

Naturally, to survive into modern times, the race has changed greatly in nature from its pioneering days, but only in the sense that it has been streamlined to suit modern thinking. For example, these days — in contrast to early Tours, when riders were forced to continue into the night to finish a stage — riders stop every day and sleep in an hotel. They are also allowed to accept assistance from helpers in team cars. However, there are still time limits to beat, and no matter how injured the riders are, they will be eliminated if they don't cross the finish line every day. Nowadays, every rider wants to retire saying he has ridden the Tour de France — although many may deny this. But that was not the case in the beginning.

Desgrange's idea — prompted by a suggestion by Géo Lefevre, a member of the staff — in 1902 was to stage a bicycle race around France the following year to publicize his sports paper *L'Auto*. But this was not everyone's cup of tea. There were many organizational problems, not least the un-made roads and the fact that the pioneers would have to continue through the night (making it impossible to be sure who was in the lead, or to know exactly where the riders were on the course).

The original Tour was advertised in *L'Auto* at the beginning of 1903 as taking place over six stages, 2,428 km and a period of 35 days. Cycle-racing was already taking its place as a major European sport. The late 1800s had seen the first event in Saint-Cloud, Paris — won by Englishman James Moore — and Europe was establishing a few classic races which exist today, such as Bordeaux–Paris, Liège–Bastogne–Liège and Paris–

Although he never rode in the Tour de France, Tour founder Henri Desgrange was an accomplished rider over shorter distances. He set the first hour record on the track on 11 May 1893 in Paris with 35 km 325m.

Englishman James Moore (right) was the first winner of a massed start race on 31 May 1868. Moore won the classic from Paris to Rouen.

Roubaix. But interest in the first Tour was not great and when with only a week to go M. Desgrange found a mere fifteen riders had entered he decided to alter the entry conditions. He cut down the duration to three weeks — from 1 July to 19 July, the same period as in 1988 — reduced the entry fee to only 20 old French francs (20p) and added prizes of 2,000 francs (£20).

The changes worked; 60 riders started in the first Tour and 21 finished. The Giants of the Road (as they were later to become known) had been discovered, for they had ridden on average 400 km to complete each stage, often by continuing into the night.

This first event was won by by little Maurice Garin, a 32-year-old chimney-sweep who was born in Italy but fortunately for the French chose to take French nationality, so the home nation started well.

It took Garin 94 hours 33 minutes to ride from Paris via Lyons, Marseilles, Toulouse, Bordeaux, Nantes and back to Paris (Ville d'Avray), winning by almost three hours. In 1987 Dublin's Stephen Roche beat the Spaniard Pedro Delgado by just 40 seconds. The following year Garin was not so popular. Although he came first again, four months after his victory the title passed to the 19-year-old Henri Cornet after the top four finishers had been disqualified for 'corruption' (which included placing tacks on the road and erecting barricades). This led to Desgrange's announcement in *L'Auto* — after just two years — of 'the death' of the Tour de France. However, he was pacified when the French Cycling Union announced its disqualifications of the riders concerned, ranging from two years for Garin to life for René Pothier.

In 1905 the problems continued — perhaps it was an indication of the Tour's future popularity — and on the opening stage from Paris to Nancy over 200lb of nails were found. All the riders had flat tyres, but no one admitted the prank and no one was ever punished.

Throughout the years French riders have always managed to do well in their own event, even though the contest has never been intentionally weighted in the home nation's favour. Louis Petit-Breton became the first man to do the double (1907/8), and since then two of the three riders who have won the race five times (see Chapter 3) have been French, while the third, Louison Bobet (a great favourite with the crowds) won three times in a row (1953–5).

Even before the First World War, riders recognized that the Tour de France was becoming THE race to win and even today accept that, while you can win other races, a stage win or final victory in the Tour de France will make you the most famous in the world.

When the Tour was resumed after the First World War there were new problems: the war had reduced the number of cars available to assist, hotels were scarce, and tragically some of the riders had been killed in combat. François Faber, the winner in 1909, had died in the Foreign Legion, and Petit-Breton (1907 and 1908) and the 1910 victor Octave Lapize were also dead.

It may seem impossible, but the race was run, and over an enormous 5,560 km — this increased distance was a momentous change that altered the face of world cycling.

'No one knows who is leading the race,' complained onlook-

Left: *Cyclists don't usually smoke, but it didn't stop Maurice Garin from winning the first Tour de France in 1903.*

This magnificent memorial to Henri Desgrange stands near the summit of the Col du Télégraphe, a 'stepping-stone' to the Galibier.

Desgrange decided to give the race leader a yellow jersey to wear.

ers. So Desgrange, after asking for suggestions about what to do, decided to give the race leader a yellow jersey to wear. Yellow, because that was the colour of the pages of *L'Auto*. *Le Maillot Jaune* was born, and it was to become the symbol of world Tours, although organizations elsewhere chose different colours for varied reasons.

The first yellow jersey was worn by Eugéne Christophe on 19 July 1919 at the start of the stage from Grenoble in France to Geneva in Switzerland. Oh, yes, the Tour de France has never worried about losing its identity by racing into other countries!

Christophe was everyone's favourite, but Belgium were to win the first Tour where the leaders wore a yellow jersey — victory going to Firmin Lambot. The hapless Frenchman was left with broken front forks on his bicycle (a catastrophe that befell him again in 1922), which he tried to repair in a black-

smith's near Valenciennes, reaching Paris finally with a deficit of over two hours and in third place overall.

Lambot's 1919 victory had continued Belgium's pre-war winning streak, and for the next four years the trend was to continue. Philippe Thijs, who had won in 1913 and 1914, bounced back in 1920 with his third victory, and with Belgian riders filling the first seven places perhaps the French felt that the Tour was not a good idea after all!

Belgium continued winning, but their lean spell was still to come and France returned to the top in 1923, when Henri Pélissier won by a mere 31 minutes. It was a sweet victory for the Frenchman, especially after so many people had said he would never win.

Ottavio Bottecchia — who had been expected to succeed against Pélissier in 1923 — took the next two races, giving Italy

To make sure the riders in the early Tours weren't tempted to cheat, secret controls were placed strategically along the route. This one, in 1927, was on a very wet Col de Peyresourde in the Pyrenees.

her first victories. In fact, even today, the Italians are not considered to be serious competitors in the Tour. They are highly paid professionals, and race for teams which have little or no commercial interest in achieving high performance in France. Only four other Italians have won the race.

The topography of France is well suited to cycle-racing, but because of the poorly surfaced roads across the mountains — if any existed at all — they provided a fearsome challenge to the Tour-men.

The Ballon d'Alsace was the first mountain to be included in the Tour, being part of the 1905 route. The 3,970-ft road in the beautiful Vosges countryside near Mulhouse was so steep that, not surprisingly, many riders were forced to walk. In these early days mountain roads were mostly tracks, used only by hill farmers, but the most famous of the climbs seen on television today emerged from the formative years of the Tour de France.

The giant among France's alpine roads is the Col du Galibier, first used in 1911 when its roughly made surfaces ended at the snowline, a height of 8,600 ft. The climb is over 32 miles and, depending on the approach, can include that of either the Col du Télégraphe (5,151 ft) or the Col du Lauteret (6,750 ft). The memorial to Henri Desgrange (who died in 1940 at seventy-five) is sited near the top of the Télégraphe. In the years when the Tour goes past here the first two riders receive a generous prize. In 1988 this was £1,500 and £500, but because the Télégraphe was omitted from the route at a late stage, the award was given on the Col du Tourmalet.

France is a beautiful country, and it is not difficult to feel why the French people are so jealous of what they have. For a racing — or touring — cyclist it is just about perfect! The Galibier is to the Alps what the Col du Tourmalet at 7,000 ft is to the Pyrenees, or Mont Ventoux (6,200 ft) to Provence, or the Puy de Dôme (4,642 ft) to the Massif Central. All have played their part in shaping the race's history.

In 1936 Desgrange handed over the Tour organization to Jacques Goddet, at that time editor of *L'Auto*, after having been forced by sickness to give up at Charleville during the race. Goddet — who is still part of the race entourage — was destined to become a legend. This amazing man, educated at Oxford, has today more than fifty races under his deerstalker or pith helmet, and although he is over eighty, his every word is respected by young rider and old journalist alike.

Working as a co-director of the race with M. Goddet was Félix Levitan. For thirty years, until M. Levitan left the organization in 1987, two Frenchmen not only steered the Tour de France but also governed the direction of world cycling for almost a third of the sport's life.

In modern times, the Société du Tour de France (briefly headed by director-general Jean-François Naquet-Radiguet in

Right: *The giant of the Alps, the Col du Galibier, always attracts many spectators, because it is on these roads that the Tour can be won — or lost. The mountain figures on the Tour route this year.*

1988) has control of a multi-million promotion, but that certainly was not so as it struggled through the leaner periods.

Only four riders have led in a race from the beginning to the end: Maurice Garin in 1903, and then in 1904 (before being disqualified); the Italian Ottavio Bottecchia in 1924; Luxembourg's Nicolas Frantz in 1928; and Belgium's Romain Maes in 1936.

There have been those who have never won the leader's jersey yet took the verdict overall after the last stage in Paris, like little Jean Robic in 1947 and Jan Janssen, the bespectacled Dutchman, in 1968.

The late Jacques Anquetil came extremely close to a win-all-the-way victory in 1961, when he led from the second part of the first day's double stage to the end. If only his team-mate, sprint specialist André Darrigade, had not won the morning session! Jacques — who died in November 1987 at fifty-three — Eddy Merckx, the legendary Belgian, and Bernard Hinault, 'the Badger', are the only riders to have won the race five times, and later you can read about these three men of men in their own chapter.

There have been others too who have won the hearts of not just the French, but all of Western Europe. Only Britain, protected from the midsummer fever of the Continent by an indifferent home media, has been kept blissfuly unaware of the

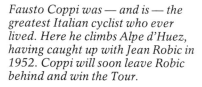

Fausto Coppi was — and is — the greatest Italian cyclist who ever lived. Here he climbs Alpe d'Huez, having caught up with Jean Robic in 1952. Coppi will soon leave Robic behind and win the Tour.

great cyclists' heroic feats. Fausto Coppi — as famous in Italy as was footballer Stanley Matthews in Britain — won the Tour twice (in 1949 and 1952), and even today the *campionnissimo* (the supreme champion) is still seen by many as the greatest rider who ever lived. Fausto (who once received a hero's welcome at London's Herne Hill stadium) died from malaria when only forty, but not before attaining an outstanding record, unrivalled in the sport until the advent of Eddy Merckx.

There is nothing better than rivalry and controversy to promote any event, and the Tour de France has left little to the imagination in either quarter during its first seventy-five years. As you will read later, it has developed so quickly in the last twenty years that it has become a runaway, with the handful of skilled men of the Société fighting desperately to keep it within bounds.

Nowadays, when an event becomes a major attraction people with views to air move in, and in the last fifteen years the Tour has become a target at which strikers demonstrate and which terrorists attack — Henri Desgrange would have been shocked. I can still smell the pungent smoke wisping in through our open windows as I, my closest friend the late David Saunders (from the *Daily Telegraph*) and Geoffrey Nicholson (now with the *Independent*) were shaken from our beds in the beautiful Pyrenean village of St Lary Soulon in 1974. Spanish terrorists had blown up a garage only a few hundred yards away, containing six Tour cars and motor-bikes. A note was delivered saying that Spanish riders would be killed on the Tourmalet, where the race was due next day, but although the road had to be cleared of felled trees, there was no further trouble.

The first time the Tour de France was forced to cancel a stage after it had begun was in Northern France, when striking workers in the industrial town of Denain blocked the road in 1982. The 73-km team time-trial came to a halt as the first teams to leave Orchies were turned around in the road. The finish town of Fontaine au Piré, one of the smallest ever used for the Tour, had been robbed of the greatest moment in its history. However, Félix Levitan, the then director, made a promise that the race would return, and so it did in 1983 with a 100-km team time-trial from Soissons. Fontaine gave the journalists a wonderful champagne party that will never be forgotten!

New rules and regulations have often altered the direction of the Tour and it was partly due to the long days caused by early starts and long road journeys in between the racing stages, with few hours to recover, that led to the riders' strike at Valence d'Agen in 1978. A huge crowd was waiting to see the Tour arrive in the town for the first time, and the produce of the area — from wine to pâté de foie gras — was spread out on long tables in the courtyard. It was going to be a pleasant stop before the race continued in the afternoon to Toulouse. Con-

There is nothing better than rivalry and controversy to promote any event.

Here are the ten away venues:

1954 – Amsterdam

1958 – Brussels

1965 – Cologne

1973 – Scheveningen

1975 – Charleroi

1978 – Leiden

1980 – Frankfurt

1982 – Basle

1987 – West Berlin

1989 – Luxembourg

tinue it did, but it was far from pleasant after Bernard Hinault had led the riders in protest over their 'work' conditions, walking over the line to boos from the disillusioned crowd. The riders, it must be said, did have a point to make, but they perhaps chose the wrong time to do it, and as things turned out the people of Valence did not have the race back for four years.

During this present decade the organizers have tried to gain support for the new title of 'Tour de France and of Europe', but in the end there is only one acceptable title, even if the race does occasionally extend its host country's borders!

Since 1903 the race has started on foreign soil nine times — the tenth coming this year in Luxembourg — including the million-pound spectacular in West Berlin in 1987. Now there are indications that the direction would like to see it start abroad every other year. For the third year, the senior management of the race has been changed, and Jean-Pierre Courcol is the new Director General. Xavier Louy left in January, and although both sides say the parting was amicable, indications are to the contrary. Jean Marie Leblanc, a journalist who has worked the Tour for many years, and who rode with BIC, the French trade team, in 1968 and 1970, is the new race director.

The race has always ended in Paris, and after the demise of the *vélodrome* at the Parc des Princes, the finish was moved to its present home, the Champs-Élysées, in 1975. The first time it ended on the wide, cobbled boulevard it was won by Frenchman Bernard Thevenet, but to many the real event was the first defeat of Eddy Merckx, who after winning five times finished second.

During the 1975 race Merckx became a hero of the French. Injured in a stupid fall as the race moved in neutral formation towards the start of the seventeenth stage (halfway up the Col du Télégraphe in the Alps), he continued to race in spite of a serious facial injury that turned out to be a fractured cheekbone.

The world champion went on, finishing every stage, shaking and looking like a Red Indian, with his white warpaint over the injury. He had won five Tours with ease; in defeat he was an equally dominant figure. The doctors disowned him publicly, over the Race radio and in the Press, as they feared he could do himself permanent damage by going on, but Merckx was in no mood for stopping! This show of heroism made the first finish on the Champs-Élysées a great and memorable occasion. The French President, Valéry Giscard d'Estaing, was also on the *Tribune d'Honneur*. What a perfect climax, with a French winner in Bernard Thevenet as well!

Merckx wore the rainbow jersey of a world champion, as for the first time in his life he had reached a finish of a Tour without the yellow 'Golden Fleece'. This was unlike his other Tours, however; for on this occasion he had returned looking human and fallible; in short, a hero like never before. 'If I had not finished this race, Thevenet's victory would not have looked as great as it surely was,' said Merckx. He was right.

Tragedies far more serious than the injury to Merckx have been sprinkled liberally through the years. Inevitably, perhaps, spectators have died watching the race after being struck by Tour vehicles. Race officials too have died, rushing to carry out their duties. Among the riders, three have succumbed during the period of the race, but only Tom Simpson has actually lost his life during the competition. Mr Tom, or Major Simpson (as the French affectionately called him) set his heart on becoming the first English-speaking rider, and more importantly, the first Englishman, to win the race, but in 1967 he died on the thirteenth stage on 13 July, little more than a kilometre from the summit of the broiling, moonscape surface of Mont Ventoux, in the centre of Provence.

Simpson had ridden the race six times before, and after taking sixth place in 1962 was determined that he could win it when he went to the start at Angers in 1967. His joking approach and his fluent understanding of French enabled his very English humour (he hailed from the Yorkshire/Nottingham borders) to be understood, even by the French. He often joked that he carried 'jam butties' in his back pockets for food.

Twenty-one years after he died in the race, Tom Simpson is still remembered by the Tour Caravan as the only Englishman to wear the leader's yellow jersey.

The Tour doctor gives Tom Simpson the 'kiss of life' as he lies stricken against the slopes of Mont Ventoux in 1967.

Left: *Jacques Goddet, a former co-director of the Tour who has followed fifty-two races, pays tribute to Tom Simpson at his memorial stone on Mont Ventoux in 1987.*

Simpson was the first British rider to break into the closely knit pedalling circus of the Tour with a realistic chance of winning, and his death from heart failure at the age of twenty-nine stunned the world of cycling. That evening in the Press room many journalists broke down and cried unashamedly when Félix Levitan broke the news.

Next day the race allowed Barry Hoban, a member of the British team, to win the stage into Sète. Hoban in the years ahead would win another seven stages in far happier circumstances.

British cyclists, inspired by Alan Gayfer (then editor of *Cycling Weekly*, Britain's oldest cycling newspaper), and lifelong journalist and publisher Peter Bryan gave enough money to erect a magnificent memorial showing the unmistakable silhouette of Simpson riding. This was set up a kilometre from the summit of Mont Ventoux, and is still visited regularly. Those who have stood there, feeling the heat and the wind hitting the stone with unrestricted violence, will understand what a lonely mountain Mont Ventoux is.

A post-mortem on Simpson revealed traces of ampheta-

All the loneliness (and courage) of the early pioneers is seen here in 1925. The unmade roads seemed to go up and up and up. . . .

mines in his blood, and although these drugs were not blamed for his death — they may have been a contributory factor — dope testing of riders became more important than it had ever been before.

Drugs in sport is an emotive subject, charged even more by the Pedro Delgado affair in last year's Tour, but nowadays all the leaders, stage winners and a random selection of riders are tested every day during the race.

It is a humiliating experience to be stripped of your clothes, especially after an exhausting eight hours in the saddle, and then be expected to face someone you do not know and pee into a small glass pot but the riders have brought this upon themselves, as over the years they have made every effort to cheat the controls. There is a tale of a rider being informed he was negative with regard to drugs, but congratulated on his pregnancy and this is not fiction!

The most famous incident of cheating came on top of Alpe d'Huez in 1978 after the little Belgian Michel Pollentier had climbed to his first yellow jersey and a stage win. However, at the control afterwards he was accused of using a plastic tube

---

Interesting Tour facts

Since 1903 the riders have covered 335,553 km (208,509 miles).

This represents a total riding time of 1 year, 9 hours, 34 minutes, 8 seconds.

9,218 riders have started, and 4,949 have finished.

Only 186 riders have worn the leader's yellow jersey.

On a clear day, the summit of the Puy de Dôme can be seen for a hundred miles. It is the giant of the Massif Centrale.

with the intention of giving a false urine sample; the happiest day of his life turned to tragedy as he was disqualified. This was a far harsher penalty than if he had given a positive test result. Then it would have been a fine and a time penalty, which would certainly have lost him the Tour but not the chance to continue.

It must be emphasized that even the simplest cold cure — often available without prescription — has a banned substance in it. Unfortunately, this means that a rider contracting any illness is now virtually doomed to retire from the race, as no leeway is allowed in the testing of samples, even if the amount of illegal substance taken is insignificant. Professional riders now want a new code of ethics drawn up, so that they may continue to practise their profession when suffer-

By now you will have gathered that the route is varied every year, the towns attracting the race by offering money and the organizers happily taking it. Wherever the race goes, though, it will always pass through the Alps and the Pyrenees, otherwise it would be like holding the Grand National without any jumps! And it is here where the crowds flock every summer to witness the clashes of the giants.

A mere glance at the Tour, wherever it is, will leave lasting memories: the noise of the cars, the speed, the colourful *peloton* of riders, the advance caravan of acrobats, the fun in the staging towns at night, with the Tour Spectacle theatre all part of the daily movement of almost three thousand people.

It is only fitting to end this brief look at the world's most demanding annual event by talking of the *Lanterne Rouge*. The last man in the Tour is remembered, so if you cannot win there's the opportunity to tell how you finished last. Believe me, in a race like the Tour de France there is no shame to finish at the back. Remember, almost half who have started the Tour de France since 1903 have never seen Paris at the end.

Chapter 2
The Performers

Pedro Delgado, the first Spanish winner of the Tour de France for fifteen years, was personally welcomed by the highest dignitaries of his country. Even at the height of his suspected doping scandal during the 1988 race, he was visited by Spain's Minister of Sport, who asked him to continue in the race for Spain. In the Tour de France it means so much to finish, and for this reason everyone felt sorry for Gerrie Knetemann from Holland, who crashed out of his thirteenth Tour — which may have been his last. There were other tales too, like the New Zealander Nathan Dahlberg, who received the call-up for his team only a few hours before the race began — and he managed to complete the race! Another Dutchman, Henk Lubberding, finally wore the leader's yellow jersey after riding the race twelve times with distinction. These are the men who have made the Tour de France what it is — the greatest race on earth.

Opposite: The 1988 Tour turned out to be a battle between Pedro Delgado (left) and a new Dutch superstar, Steven Rooks.

Whichever way you view the Tour de France, it is by far the biggest and most famous cycle race in the world. The other thousand or so races listed on the world calendar each season have only followed the trends set by this remarkable event.

The Tour's history shows that it has dominated the French way of life for three-quarters of a century. For example, no French politician would dare campaign or call a general election in July — the risk of a low turnout would be too great, especially if a Frenchman was leading the Tour de France!

The Tour has to be commercially minded to carry on and needs to earn £7,000,000 a year from sponsorship, advertising opportunities and entry fees to survive. Such a large turnover gives the race a place in the French economy; for as well as earning money for the sponsors, it also promotes the French countryside and heritage to the world at large.

There is, of course, a price to be paid for these benefits: for example, the inconvenience to other road-users is enormous, as wherever the race goes roads are closed for many hours before the riders pass by to prevent spectators from blocking the route. The narrow roads in the mountains are sometimes closed as early as six in the morning, some nine hours before the race arrives. Since 1984 there has been the added complication of the new women's Tour (see Chapter 10) which precedes the men's race by two or more hours.

But despite this, the gains to France outweigh any difficulties. It is no exaggeration to say that the race is seen on television throughout the world, with most of the European countries offering live coverage. Outside Europe, cycling in general — with the Tour de France leading the way via the small screen — is also gaining in popularity. In Colombia, where cycling is now the most popular sport in the country (thanks largely to the success of Luis Herrera in the Tour de France), the public get eight hours a day saturation coverage, and

Right: *The Tour approaches. The bunch looks compact, but at any moment an attack could alter all that.*

Below: *The Tour even has its own flag, and every day at the official start a gendarme signals that the stage has begun.*

Australia, Japan, the United States and Canada are all kept up to date.

However, times have changed since M. Desgrange and his staff originally thought of the Tour: its future now depends on a substantial income achieved by its saleability. In the last three years the Tour has become more conscious of selling itself, and its image now contains much more 'hype' than in the 1970s.

The achievements of riders from far-off countries such as Colombia, America, Canada, New Zealand and Australia have created a great deal of interest, helping to bridge the gap between them and the European countries who accepted the sport many years ago.

Closer to home, Ireland and Britain are enjoying a surge of interest greater than ever before, following the success of riders like Robert Millar and the Irishmen Sean Kelly and Stephen Roche. And elsewhere, riders such as Phil Anderson from Australia, Luis Herrera from Colombia, Raul Alcala from Mexico, Steve Bauer and Alex Stieda from Canada and Greg LeMond and Andy Hampsten from the United States, have all awakened interest back home, where traditional sports have never included cycle-racing.

For years cycling has been a relatively introverted sport, and its stars have never managed to attain the salaries enjoyed by the luminaries of golf, tennis or the new television attraction, snooker. However, in recent years the prize-lists have not just doubled but quadrupled. For example, until recently the major classics — these are always single-day races — carried a first prize of less than £1,000. Now the value of the Paris–Roubaix race (also organized by the Société du Tour de France) has gone up overnight to £13,000 after a new sponsor was found. The prize-list for last year's Tour de France was £720,690, double what it was three years previously. Later we shall examine how the money is divided among the many various competitions within the race framework. Although the Tour can have only one winner, there are many ways to pick up prize money over a distance which varies annually between three thousand and four thousand kilometres.

First, it is important to understand the race itself. In company with a small, faithful band of British journalists and commentators, I have been following the Tour for many years, and whatever your criticisms, you can never fault its tremendous detailed organization, the equivalent of arranging a four-yearly world tournament every year!

Each day the 3,000 accredited Tour followers have to be moved on, and hotels and special facilities found to cater for the needs of so many diverse people. Tremendous organization is required to house the Press and the general media, as well as the race 'caravan' that precedes the event by some hours, and which you can read about in Chapter 7.

The equivalent of arranging a four-yearly world tournament every year!

The Tour is so big that special facilities have to be granted by governments of the host countries, such as the arrival of customs officers to check papers the day before the race starts, so that on the morrow it can pass unhindered across neighbouring borders. The movement of this complete Tour 'family' makes the Tour de France unique, and newcomers learn the house rules fast or find they are thrown out of the race.

How can anyone be thrown off a public road? Without any difficulty at all if you lose the famous Tour plaque (a paper sticker these days) from your car — then you will never be allowed there in the first place, such is the strictness of the road-closure orders.

The race is escorted by the Gendarmerie Nationale, and a finer bunch of motor-cyclists would be hard to find. The Tour riders may be skilled descenders in the mountains, but even

Immaculate in their turnout, brilliant at their job. The Gendarmerie Nationale prepare for their day in the saddle.

they would have trouble matching the expertise of the hand-picked police outriders. The police have an enormous task to guarantee the safety of their live 'cargo' and the motor-cycle escort needs both a knowledge of crowd control and general escort duties, and a perfect understanding of the constantly changing pattern of the race. They need to know instinctively where to place themselves when riding alongside the cyclists, so they do not affect their progress or — even worse — spoil an opportunity to attack by being in the way.

The police are controlled by a commander who rides in a chauffeur-driven car about two kilometres in front of the leading rider(s). He will constantly be using the telephone or short-wave radio to make sure the route ahead is clear, and his small army of police outriders are always in the right place.

The Tour moves fast, riders often reaching speeds of 70 mph, so there is never time for complacency — is it surprising

An hour or more behind, the riders toil, while up front the Publicity Caravan entertains.

that the rule book for the drivers and followers of the Tour is now many pages thick?

For example, if you drive ahead of the race in a Press car, you must drive on the right and allow other vehicles free passage on the left. But if you drive behind the race, you must drive on the left with the team cars immediately on the right. All cars accredited to follow the race itself must be equipped with a Tour short-wave radio receiver, and this is checked and tested by a Tour official before they are given the vehicle's race plaque. The receiver is used to listen to a continual flow of messages from the race, which keeps everybody informed of the happenings around the riders: crashes, flat tyres, attacks, leaders, time gaps are all given within seconds of occurring.

Radio messages — often delivered at fever pitch — also direct the progress of the cars themselves. For example, if cars moving slowly ahead of the race hear that the riders have accelerated or there is a town ahead with narrow streets (which may take 150 cars a while to negotiate before the race itself arrives) they will naturally increase their own speed.

Many people — including the Tour organization — are worried that there are too many cars and motor-bikes accompanying the race, and are concerned about the riders' safety. The organizers have resorted to putting up an aeroplane so that the radio signals can be bounced off equipment in the plane and received by cars driving up to 100 km ahead. This is done in the hope that many cars will go ahead, rest and just listen!

Most of the Tour's income comes from commercial backing of the different competitions and not from the publicity caravan that travels ahead. These vehicles are not given the Tour radio and are never allowed near the riders. A policeman rides behind to ensure they keep well ahead. Every vehicle in the publicity caravan pays anything from £1,000 a day for the chance to be seen (and sell or give away its products!) by upward of 750,000 spectators on the roadside daily. No other sports event offers such an opportunity. The major sponsors — those backing the competition and various classifications, such as the sprint or climbing competitions — naturally pay a lot more, and even the cycling teams do not ride for free. The entry price (which can vary) begins at around £30,000, although this goes mainly towards the cost of housing the team.

Like all good businesses, the Société du Tour de France varies its price to suit its purchaser, so sponsorship, television rights and entry fees are all a matter for negotiation.

The French sporting daily *L'Équipe*, the successor of *L'Auto*, and *Le Parisien-Libéré* are still the main supporters of the race, but the Société has been formed as a separate company, operating (hopefully) on a profit-making basis. In 1987 the company moved in to a new building made of smoked glass and painted in blue and white in the Paris suburb of Issy-les-Moulineaux, near the Eiffel Tower. Its occupancy of the fifth floor in such a modernistic building presents a great contrast to the organization's early days in the backstreet office of *L'Auto* in the Faubourg Montmartre in Paris.

The number of people in the organization are relatively few, considering the amount of work involved. The men in charge of the technical day-to-day problems are Xavier Louy, Richard Marillier and Albert Bouvet. These three have worked on many Tours, and are in control of technical decisions and route planning. Richard Marillier was formerly the French national trainer, and Albert Bouvet was himself a great rider, having taken part in the Tour six times between 1954 and 1962.

In addition, the Press are looked after by Claude and Philippe Sudres, while in 1987 Bernard Hinault, a five-times winner, joined the team. Between them they do a remarkable job in bringing the race to fruition each year.

To link so many French towns into a complex route is a feat in itself, but to help each town subsequently to plan its own special piece of publicity is an added problem which the organization faces with enthusiasm. For the town concerned, the race's visit is an important occasion, while the fact that it will move on the next day detracts not at all from the celebrations and publicity stunts.

The Tour also brings its own theatre, and in 1987 introduced

Upward of 750,000 spectators on the roadside daily.

the 'biggest disco in the world' which took almost two days to erect! At night the Tour Spectacular fills the town square with comedians, singers and other fairground attractions. All this creates a special atmosphere in towns that otherwise would often be deathly silent by nine. When the Tour is in town there is little hope of finding a bed for the night within a radius of 100 km unless you are lucky and manage to pick up a cancellation.

A Tour route is always announced in October, and by that time most of the big hotels will have already been booked by the organization. Following the announcement, the journalists — who will have been waiting for details of the closely guarded route — will spend the next day on the phone ringing their favourite hotels (most journalists strike up friendships with the hoteliers over the years, and always try to go back when the race next passes by), to ensure that they too have beds.

The race, as you may have gathered by now, is a complex moving unit and the official Tour pass, worn proudly around the neck by all followers, is also an identity disc that helps in many situations.

At the end of every stage the race has a *permanence* — a central headquarters — where a police station is open to record all incidents, including any accidents which have happened during the stage. Outside in the car-park is a mobile bank that handles all the foreign exchange of the many nations present and accepts the receipts from the roadside sellers of the publicity caravan out on the route all day.

There is also a complete medical back-up system for the riders, a hand-picked team of medical men, led by Dr Gérard Porte, who understand the special needs of athletes. Dr Porte watches over his flock from an open-topped car and is quickly on hand in the event of a crash or the call from a rider who feels unwell.

Above all, he understands the mentality of a rider who may be injured and sick, but who does not want to give up his daily torture in return for a warm hospital bed. Only under exceptional circumstances would Dr Porte call the rider out of the race. Instead he or his team will offer tablets, dressings and injections on the move, the administration of which demands a special skill in itself. They are handicapped too by the banned list of drugs that could disqualify the rider.

In the event of a serious crash — which is more likely to happen in the mountains, where riders have on a number of occasions left the road and sailed many metres down the slopes — Dr Porte can call on helicopters to lift the victims quickly to hospital. The most famous incident of this kind was in 1960, when Roger Rivière (already winner of three stages) raced into the beautiful Tarn Gorges only to disappear off the Col de Perjuret. Earlier in the day Rivière — one of France's most accomplished cyclists, and still only in his second Tour —

had predicted he would win the race. As it turned out, his injuries were so serious that he never raced again, and died only a few years later. It was a historic Tour in other ways, because the riders had stopped in Colombey-les-Deux-Églises to meet the President, General Charles de Gaulle.

These days the riders have things very much easier than was the case in the opening Tours, although they may not always think so. Before the race starts each one is given a thorough medical examination at the Permanence, and after that their own team will take over their well-being.

Many people watching the race on television for the first time ask the question: 'Why isn't the winner of the race the first rider to cross the finish line in Paris?' Well, this would only work if the riders really did set off as a group, restarting every day in the positions they finished the evening before, and arriving back in Paris separated by many hours.

There would be no spectacle for the crowds to see — just one rider rolling in three hours — or even days — ahead of the next. No, the only practical way to find the winner of the Tour de France

Above: *A pain in the knee? No problem for the doctors of the Tour.*

Left: *Riders fight all odds to keep in the race, and the doctors understand. Here Colombia's Rafaël Acevedo receives treatment for a head wound.*

is to log each rider's daily time and publish a daily list of standings (known as the Overall Classification). The next morning the riders all set off together again (except in the case of individual time-trials, where riders are timed separately), and have to try and win back time lost by leaving those ahead of them in the classification behind them on the stage. Riders finishing in the same group are always given the same time, with the man at the back of the bunch — be it four or two hundred strong — receiving the same time as the winner, although in reality they may be more than thirty seconds apart. This may seem strange, but is common sense really. You cannot allow two hundred riders to commit suicide trying to save seconds by racing flat out for the front on narrow, twisting roads. But if a gap opens in the big bunch and a separate time can be given, then it will be. For this reason you will always see the main contenders finishing in the front half of the field although they may not be interested in the stage win itself. Bearing this in mind, let us look at the competitions.

The Yellow Jersey

This is the most coveted of all world symbols, except perhaps for the rainbow jersey of a world champion. At the end of any given day the rider who has covered the course in the shortest time to this point is the overall race leader and wears the *maillot jaune* on the following stage. (For a full list of all the winners of the Tour, see Appendix, pp. 154-155.)

Over the years the battle for the yellow jersey has produced some close finishes in Paris. The five mostly hotly contested Tours are shown opposite.

Five hotly contested Tours

1968, when Dutchman Jan Janssen beat Herman Van Springel (B) by 38 seconds after 4,684 km.

1987, when Stephen Roche (Ireland) beat Pedro Delgado of Spain by 40 seconds after 4,230 km.

1977, when Bernard Thevenet from France beat Hennie Kuiper of Holland by 48 seconds after 4,099 km.

1964, when French ace Jacques Anquetil beat arch-rival Raymond Poulidor by 55 seconds after 4,504 km.

1966, when Lucien Aimar beat Jan Janssen by 67 seconds after 4,323 km.

The biggest margin of victory was in the very first race in 1903 when Maurice Garin beat Lucien Pothier by 2 hours 49 min 45 sec after 2,428 km.

The three most wanted men in the race — at least while they wear the leaders' jerseys. From left to right, Sean Kelly (points), overall leader Laurent Fignon; and King of the Mountains (Lucien Van Impe).

Another British Tour regular is Sue Thompson, who recently married professional cyclist Alan Gornall. As Sue Thompson, she had ridden the Tour for the last three years.

Sean Kelly demonstrating the vital tactic of conserving energy.

Eddy Planckaert of Belgium won his first green jersey last year.

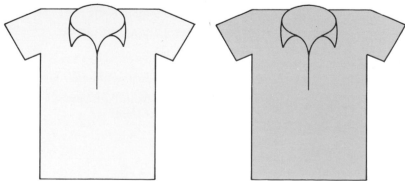

Yellow Jersey

Green Jersey

Polka Dot Jersey

Stephen Roche suffers in a time-trial on Mont Ventoux in 1987. His team car, with mechanic Patrick Valcks out on the roof, is ready for any situation that requires their help.

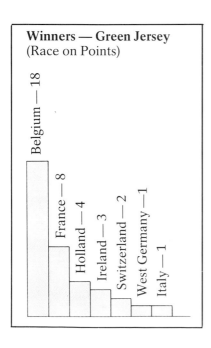

Winners — Green Jersey
(Race on Points)

Belgium — 18
France — 8
Holland — 4
Ireland — 3
Switzerland — 2
West Germany — 1
Italy — 1

The Green Jersey

The *maillot vert* is the second most important jersey to go for, and favours the consistent high finishers in the daily stages of the race.

Although in the early days the race itself was sometimes decided on points and not time, nowadays the points race is a separate competition.

Every day the first 25 riders to finish the stage are awarded points and the rider with the most points at the start of any stage wears the Green Jersey. This competition is the target of the brave sprinters who generally fear the mountains because of lack of climbing ability (which means they can rarely ever hope to win the yellow jersey). They work hard to amass a big lead before the hilly stages, but they are not always successful.

The points competition was introduced in 1953, and here are the winners to date:

The Green Jersey Honours List

1953 – Fritz Schaer (Switz)	1971 – Eddy Merckx (B)
1954 – Ferdi Kubler (Switz)	1972 – Eddy Merckx (B)
1955 – Stan Ockers (B)	1973 – Herman Van Springel (B)
1956 – Stan Ockers (B)	
1957 – Jean Forestier (F)	1974 – Patrick Sercu (B)
1958 – Jean Graczyk (F)	1975 – Rik Van Linden (B)
1958 – André Darrigade (F)	1976 – Freddy Maertens (B)
1959 – André Darrigade (F)	1977 – Jacques Esclassan (F)
1960 – Jean Graczyk (F)	1978 – Freddy Maertens (B)
1961 – André Darrigade (F)	1979 – Bernard Hinault (F)
1962 – Rudi Altig (WG)	1980 – Rudy Pevenage (B)
1963 – Rik Van Looy (B)	1981 – Freddy Maertens (B)
1964 – Jan Janssen (Hol)	1982 – Sean Kelly (Ire)
1965 – Jan Janssen (Hol)	1983 – Sean Kelly (Ire)
1966 – Willy Planckaert (B)	1984 – Frank Hoste (B)
1967 – Jan Janssen (Hol)	1985 – Sean Kelly (Ire)
1968 – Franco Bitossi (I)	1986 – Eric Vanderaerden (B)
1969 – Eddy Merckx (B)	1987 – Jean Paul Van Poppel (Hol)
1970 – Walter Godefroot (B)	1988 – Eddy Planckaert (B)

Of those still competing, Sean Kelly could become the first person to win the competition four times if he wins in 1989. Britain's highest-placed finisher was Yorkshire's Barry Hoban, who came third overall in 1974.

The Polka-Dot Jersey

This jersey is the real eyecatcher! It is a white jersey with red spots, and it is awarded daily to the rider who has accumulated the highest points total on the designated hills or mountains. The competition is often referred to as the 'King of the Mountains' or 'Grand Prix of the Mountains'. The organizers categorize the climbs depending on severity from fourth (the lowest), where the first three riders over the top score points; to third, where the first five riders score; to second, where the first ten score; and finally to first, where twelve score, and the 'hors' category (the steepest climbs) where fifteen riders score points. This is considered the most romantic of the competitions, as the ability to climb the high mountains is the most desired quality of a stage-race cyclist, and it is where the crowds pack in dense numbers to cheer them by.

Sean Kelly has been officially the world number one since rankings began in 1983.

Charly Gaul from Luxembourg became known as the Angel of the Mountains and Spain's Federico Bahamontes earned the title the Eagle of Toledo.

This competition began in 1933, and here are the winners.

The Polka-Dot Jersey Honours List

1933 – Vicente Trueba (Sp)	1958 – Federico Bahamontes (Sp)	1973 – Pedro Torres (Sp)
1934 – René Vietto (F)	1959 – Federico Bahamontes (Sp)	1974 – Domingo Perurena (Sp)
1935 – Felicien Vervaecke (B)	1960 – Imerio Massignan (I)	1975 – Lucien Van Impe (B)
1936 – Julian Berrendero (Sp)	1961 – Imerio Massignan (I)	1976 – Giancarlo Bellini (I)
1937 – Felicien Vervaecke (B)	1962 – Federico Bahamontes (Sp)	1977 – Lucien Van Impe (B)
1938 – Gino Bartali (I)	1963 – Federico Bahamontes (Sp)	1978 – Mariano Martinez (F)
1939 – Sylvere Maes (B)	1964 – Federico Bahamontes (Sp)	1979 – Giovanni Battaglin (I)
1947 – Pierre Brambilla (I)	1965 – Julio Jimenez (Sp)	1980 – Raymond Martin (F)
1948 – Gino Bartali (I)	1966 – Julio Jimenez (Sp)	1981 – Lucien Van Impe (B)
1949 – Fausto Coppi (I)	1967 – Julio Jiminez (Sp)	1982 – Bernard Vallet (F)
1950 – Louison Bobet (F)	1968 – Aurelio Gonzalez (Sp)	1983 – Lucien Van Impe (B)
1951 – Raphael Geminiani (F)	1969 – Eddy Merckx (B)	1984 – Robert Millar (Scotland)
1952 – Fausto Coppi (I)	1970 – Eddy Merckx (B)	1985 – Luis Herrera (Col)
1953 – Jesus Lorono (Sp)	1971 – Lucien Van Impe (B)	1986 – Bernard Hinault (F)
1954 – Federico Bahamontes (Sp)	1972 – Lucien Van Impe (B)	1987 – Luis Herrera (Col)
1955 – Charly Gaul (Lux)		1988 – Stephen Rooks (Hol)
1956 – Charly Gaul (Lux)		
1957 – Gastone Nencini (I)		

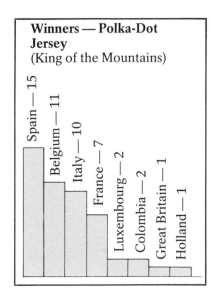

Winners — Polka-Dot Jersey
(King of the Mountains)

Spain — 15
Belgium — 11
Italy — 10
France — 7
Luxembourg — 2
Colombia — 2
Great Britain — 1
Holland — 1

Federico Bahamontes and Lucien Van Impe, now both retired, hold the record with six wins each. Scotland's Robert Millar, who won in 1984, is the only English-speaking rider to win. Last year Stephen Rooks became the first Dutchman to win the title.

Red Jersey

This competition also favours the sprinters in the race and is contested every day at any number of pre-designated points along the route — usually in villages, to add to the spectacle.

The first three riders across the line each time score points and the rider with the most aggregate points at the end of each day is given a red jersey.

To make this competition more appealing points are also awarded towards the green jersey competition, which means contenders hoping to win the green jersey will have to take an interest in a less attractive sprint series. Also, the organizers may offer small time bonuses to the first three — say, 10, 6 and 2 seconds — which are deducted from the overall time in the yellow jersey competition. This means that the actual race leaders are sometimes forced to take an interest in a competition they would normally ignore.

Red Jersey

Performance Jersey

This multi-coloured jersey, which is made up from fragments of all the other jersey designs, is the target for riders doing well in all the race's special competitions. The first 25 riders in the yellow, green, red and polka dot jersey classifications gain points in each competition, beginning at 25 points for the leader to one point for twenty-fifth place.

The highest total from the four competitions marks the leader of the performance classification. For example, a rider who is first in all four classifications would have 100 points in the performance classification. This is a complicated competition which may be withdrawn next year, as the organizers follow their new simplification policy.

Team Race

The teams also qualify for their own competition, and all the members of any one team leading the race with the shortest time at any stopover point will be given yellow hats to wear.

The individual times of the first three riders in each team to finish each stage are added together to discover the team leaders on overall time.

Performance Jersey

The winning teams since 1903			
1903 France	1921 La Sportive	1935 Belgium	1956 Belgium
1904 France	1922 Peugeot	1936 Belgium	1957 France
1905 Peugeot	1923 Auto-Moto	1937 France	1958 Belgium
1906 Peugeot	1924 Auto-Moto	1938 Belgium	1959 Belgium
1907 Peugeot	1925 Auto-Moto	1939 Belgium	1960 France
1908 Peugeot	1926 Auto-Moto	1947 Italy	1961 France
1909 Alcyon	1927 Thomann	1948 Belgium	1962 St Raphaël
1910 Alcyon	1928 Alycon	1949 Italy	1963 St Raphaël
1911 Alcyon	1929 Alycon	1950 Belgium	1964 Pelforth
1912 Alcyon	1930 France	1951 France	1965 Kas
1913 Peugeot	1931 Belgium	1952 Italy	1966 Kas
1914 Peugeot	1932 Italy	1953 Holland	1967 France
1919 La Sportive	1933 France	1954 Switzerland	1968 Spain
1920 La Sportive	1934 France	1955 France	1969 Faema

1970 Salvarani	1975 GAN—Mercier	1980 Miko—Mercier	1985 La Vie Claire
1971 Bic	1976 Kas	1981 Peugeot—Esso	1986 La Vie Claire
1972 GAN—Mercier	1977 TI—Raleigh	1982 Coop—Mercier	1987 Système U
1973 Bic	1978 Miko—Mercier	1983 TI—Raleigh	1988 PDM
1974 Kas	1979 Renault—Gitane	1984 Renault—Elf	

The team competition has varied between nations and professional trade teams, depending on which format the organizers decided to use. Since 1969 the team race has been between the trade teams.

These are the main competitions that form the backbone of the race, but in any year the organizers are likely to add more if a sponsor has money to spend!

To complicate matters further, all the competitions' jerseys must be worn, so if a rider is already wearing the yellow jersey as leader but is also in front in the points competition, then the second rider in the points competition will have to wear the green jersey.

Prizes

The next question, and one that is often asked, is 'What do they win?'

For no particular reason, the prize-list is very rarely published in the general newspapers or magazines reporting the Tour, although it is not a secret. In fact, it makes up a 10-page booklet which is given to the riders and all who are interested.

There are many ways to win money in the Tour de France, and with the competitions above in mind, here is a selection of awards. The prize money is in French francs (dividing by ten will give the approximate sterling amount at current rates of exchange). The prizes are likely to be even higher in 1989.

Yellow Jersey Competition
Final winner

A studio worth	190,000F
Cash	500,000F
Diamond route	500,000F
Peugeot car	118,000F
Total:	1,308,000F

The Diamond Route is a silver plaque in the shape of France with the route of the race traced in diamonds!

2nd –	350,000F
3rd –	175,000F
4th –	120,000F
5th –	100,000F
6th –	50,000F
7th –	35,000F
8th –	25,000F
9th –	22,000F

etc, to hundredth place which is 1,500F.

For the first half of the route, every day a rider wears the leader's yellow jersey he receives 2,500F; after the halfway stage the price drops to 1,500F.

Green Jersey Competition

1st – 40,000F	3rd – 5,000F
2nd – 20,000F	

Every day the table leader receives 1,600F and the second 800F.

Polka-Dot Jersey
Prizes for being first over the mountains range from 3,000F for a hors category climb to 600F for a fourth category. The final winners receive:
1st – 18,000F
2nd – 8,000F
3rd – 4,000F

For the daily leader up until halfway – 500F

Afterwards until the finish – 800F

The Performance Jersey
1st – 20,000F
2nd – 10,000F

For the daily leader – 1,500F.

Daily Stage Awards
1st – A Peugeot car worth 45,000F
Silver tracing of route 20,000F
Total: 65,000F

2nd – 14,000F   3rd – 8,000F
4th – 6,000F   5th – 5,000F

etc down to 65th place which is 200F.

In 1988 a new prize was awarded in memory of Jacques Anquetil. This was called the Prix Jacques Anquetil, given to the rider wearing the yellow jersey the most days — 100,000F.

The total prize list in 1988 was 7,567,250F.

The Teams

The Tour de France field is made up of professional riders who are grouped together in trade teams. Amateur riders may take part, but few nations have the strength at amateur level or the opportunity to prepare properly for the race because of the difference between amateur and professional racing distances. Professional riders are more used to cycling for much longer — perhaps over eight hours in a day — while amateur riders rarely race more than five hours daily. Without the correct training races, amateur riders would be unlikely to keep up with the extra daily distance of the Tour. The race entry is by invitation, but any company which is prepared to spend up to £3,500,000 a year running a team will usually have the riders capable of winning the Tour in their line-up.

The teams are composed of nine or ten riders (the number will vary, and it was nine last year), who are looked after by two or three masseurs, mechanics, doctors and two managers, including the overall manager known as the Directeur Sportif. In each team there is always a leader and occasionally two, but rarely more.

The Tour de France is essentially a team race, with the team always treating its leader as the man they expect to win overall, giving him the attention that a worker bee pays a queen. On rare occasions, a very strong team might have two members capable of winning the race, but in such a case the riders themselves may come into conflict, splitting the loyalties of their team-mates if both command winning positions.

If the leader falls the team will wait and help him back to the safety of the field. If he punctures, he can expect a new wheel or a bike from his team-mate, so that no time is lost. However, he is expected to display his ability when required, and to win either the day's stage or the race itself. When the pressure goes on he must be in the thick of the action, earning the confidence of his team, so that they keep on helping him.

Joaquim Agostinho was Portugal's greatest rider and a favourite in the Tour de France. He was tragically killed when a dog ran in front of him in the Tour of the Algarve.

Should the leader win the race, by tradition he will give practically all his prize money to his team. In 1987 Stephen Roche won £100,000, which was shared among the team. The winner's own fortune will be earned later in appearance and other contracts.

The helpers in the team are called *domestiques*, and they are often seen scurrying among the team cars which follow the race, collecting water and food and taking it back up to their leader. Do not think that being a *domestique* is an easy life — it most certainly is not. In order to keep their leader fresh for the serious business, the *domestiques* often have to work twice as hard as their leader to keep him in a winning position without using too much energy, and if they fail they are usually replaced next season.

Such are the demands of the Tour de France with its mountains, its specialist time-trials (these are where the team leaders really must excel) and its long, flat road race stages, that only a handful of riders are born with the ability required to win the Tour. Sooner or later their talent blossoms, and that is when they earn the privilege of being a protected rider.

'Penalties'

When the field in the Tour de France can be spread over hours on any stage, refereeing the race is an unenviable task, yet to be appointed to the race as a *commissaire* is undoubtedly a highlight of any official's career.

There are surprisingly few commissaires and judges on the Tour de France, despite the high monetary stakes for the riders. To combat the shortage of officials, there is a rule book with penalties many pages thick, and offences are punished in a number of ways.

These can range from cash fines to time penalties or even disqualification. The riders, by the way, think they know all the tricks, but sometimes the commissaires know better!

Here are some examples, with the fines in French francs. In every case they are the maximum penalties.

Late in signing-on — 110F.

Taking momentary shelter behind a car — Disqualification.

Collusion between rival competitors — 3750F and disqualification.

Taking food when not allowed — 75F and disqualification.

Modification of race number — Disqualification.

Not wearing leader's jersey — Refused the start.

Not attending prize ceremony at end of day — 1100F and forfeiture of prizes won.

Chapter 3
The Supermen

Every decade or so a sport — any sport — produces a competitor whose performances stand head and shoulders above the rest. Despite the outstanding ability of others, sooner or later along comes someone who can do it all better — no matter what the odds against may be. He (or she) is the champion born to win. There are three such champions born out of the Tour de France. Three champions of separate generations, who have broken many a heart as they have raced to five Tour victories.

To win even a stage in the Tour de France is the lifetime's ambition of most professional riders, and to win the race itself is a dream that is realized by very few. To win it more than once puts the rider in a special category.

Five Wins
Jacques Anquetil (F)
    1957, 1961, 1962, 1963, 1964
Eddy Merckx (B)
    1969, 1970, 1971, 1972, 1974
Bernard Hinault (F)
    1978, 1979, 1981, 1982, 1985

Three Wins
Philippe Thijs (B)
    1913, 1914, 1920
Louison Bobet (F)
    1953, 1954, 1955

Two Wins
Lucien Petit-Breton (F)
    1907, 1908
Firmin Lambot (B)
    1919, 1922
Ottavio Bottecchia (I)
    1924, 1925
Nicolas Frantz (Lux)
    1927, 1928
André Leducq (F)
    1930, 1932
Antonin Magne (F)
    1931, 1934
Sylvère Maes (B)
    1936, 1939
Gino Bartali (I)
    1938, 1948
Fausto Coppi (I)
    1949, 1952
Bernard Thevenet (F)
    1975, 1977
Laurent Fignon (F)
    1983, 1984

If a cyclist has been fortunate enough to win the race, can he ever persuade his body to face its rigours once again? Can he undergo its physical and mental stress in order to prove that a man can repeat his exploits of the past?

Great champions in any sport are single-minded people with an unquenchable thirst for victory. Aided by this passion, and by their ability, they apply themselves exclusively to win, and win, and keep on winning.

Before we look at these three men who share fifteen victories in the Tour de France between them, look at the scroll of honour of riders with two or more wins.

Currently, the Frenchman Laurent Fignon is the only rider with two wins to be still competing, although injury has prevented him from finding the form that won him the race in 1983 and 1984. It is therefore unlikely that the record of the Big Three will be equalled during the next decade.

The Big Three

Jacques Anquetil
'Maître' Jacques Anquetil really was the master of the big stage races. This bold Norman with the famous barrel-shaped chest which seemed capable of holding more air than normal possessed a quality that made him the finest rider of his time. Anquetil could race alone against the clock better than anyone else, and this was the rare talent that paved his route to five Tour wins.

In November 1987 France was stunned by Anquetil's death from cancer at the age of only fifty-three. This very individual man, with his fixed views on the sport and on life in general, showed his characteristic courage when, instead of undergoing major surgery for his illness, he continued working as a television commentator on the Tour de France without a word about his condition. Four months later he was dead.

Jacques Anquetil continued working as a television commentator and newspaper columnist in the 1987 Tour de France, even though he knew he was seriously ill.

Jacques Anquetil — Career Record

Name: Jacques Anquetil
Born: Mont-Saint-Aignan, 8.1.1934
Died: Rouen, 18.11.1987
Professional: 1954–69
Principal Victories:
Five Tours de France, competed eight times, winning 16 stages.
Two Tours of Italy (1960, 1964). Won six stages.
Tour of Spain (1963). Won one stage.
Paris–Nice five times.
World Hour Record holder in 1956.
GP des Nations time-trial — nine wins.
Ghent–Wevelgem 1964.
Bordeaux–Paris 1965.
Liège–Bastogne–Liège 1966.

Anquetil's Five Tour Results

1957
1. Jacques Anquetil (F) 133 hours 44 min 42 sec
2. Marcel Janssens (B) at (i.e. plus) 14 min 56 sec
3. Adolf Christian (Austria) at 17 min 20 sec
4. Jean Forestier (F) at 18 min 2 sec
5. Jesus Lorono (Sp) at 20 min 17 sec
6. Gastone Nencini (I) at 26 min 3 sec

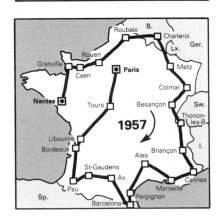

Anquetil retired on 27 December 1969 after a farewell track race in Antwerp, Belgium, and never rode a bicycle again. Instead he retired to his beautiful château near Rouen, spending all his time working the farm, indulging his passion for driving the machinery and watching the passage of the wildfowl on migration through Normandy. He retained an interest in cycling and its politics and acted as the course director for Paris–Nice, a race he had won five times. In 1987 Ireland's Sean Kelly went one better to make it six, and Anquetil was the first to toast him in champagne.

As often happens, Anquetil became more popular *after* his retirement. His arch-rival Raymond Poulidor — who often enjoyed a game of poker with him — said on Anquetil's death: 'Jacques won all the races, but I got all the cheers.'

Anquetil's smooth pedalling and streamlined position on a bicycle made it look as though he was an integral part of his machine. Even today, over thirty years after he turned professional, his style does not look dated or out of place. Everybody in Normandy recognized that the young Anquetil was special, and hoped that his performances would bring the smile back to Norman faces after nearby Brittany had produced a three-times winner in Louison Bobet.

The passing of the Jacques Anquetil and Raymond Poulidor era is still mourned in France. Here the two great Frenchmen ride side by side on the Col du Galibier in 1966.

So, at twenty-three and with his time-trialling ability already well known from his victories in France's Grand Prix des Nations (the most coveted classic individual test in the world), the young Norman went to the start line of his first Tour at Nantes in 1957. In spite of his youth, he lacked nothing in confidence, and had even refused to ride on the same team as Louison Bobet, knowing that Bobet would be the protected rider and Anquetil almost certainly a *domestique*, or at best the second choice if Bobet failed. The problem was finally solved when a young French team was brought together; Bobet was given his own squad, although ironically he did not in fact ride in the end. This left Anquetil, a member of the younger squad, to carry the hopes of France to victory.

Maître Jacques soon made his mark and won the third stage, the 134 km from Caen to his hometown of Rouen. Even then, though, the time-gain was not enough to take the yellow jersey away from his team-mate René Privat. That pleasure came two days later in Charleroi, Belgium, with Bobet in the crowd to see it happen! The only surprise was that Anquetil had taken the lead during the road-race stages, when he was expected to be making his moves in the individual time-trials. Instead he moved even farther ahead by winning the mountain time-trial on Montjuich Hill in Barcelona, followed by another time-trial victory between Bordeaux and Limbourne, finally winning his first Tour by almost fifteen minutes. Anquetil beat Marcel Janssens from Belgium and the Austrian Adolf Christian. The young French team had proved a point, too, winning twelve of the possible twenty-three stages!

The following year Anquetil retired sick in the Jura mountains, leaving victory to Charly Gaul from Luxembourg. The brilliant climber seemed to be inspired by the cold, wet weather in the mountains, while Anquetil, still worried about his French rivals Bobet and Raphael Geminiani, decided to stop, and abandon the race. However, he was back again the next year, 1959, determined to meet the challenge, which was more from his team-mates than from others. Apart from 'Gem' and Bobet, there was another challenger to the superiority of Anquetil that year; great things were being expected from Roger Rivière.

Rivière was only twenty-three — the same age as Anquetil on his first appearance — and came to the Tour having beaten the latter's world hour record on the track. That victory made him the first rider to exceed 47 km per hour.

Anquetil responded predictably: 'I will ride against Roger Rivière,' he declared, undaunted by the known ability of the newcomer.

Rivière, also the winner of the last two world pursuit titles, showed his natural gift for pure speed by beating Anquetil in both time-trials in the tour, but Jacques eventually finished third. That was one place ahead of his rival, and the only time he was to reach Paris without actually winning the Tour. The race was won by Spanish climbing star Federico Bahamontes, and although Anquetil was only 5 minutes 5 seconds behind, significantly Rivière was just 12 seconds behind him.

The next year should have been a vintage race, but instead it was a disaster for Rivière. Anquetil, having won the Tour of Italy, decided not to contest the 1960 Tour de France. This left the way open for Rivière, who was on course to win the race when a crash ended his promising career almost before it had really begun.

Roger Rivière was less than two minutes behind the Italian Gastone Nencini and had his favourite time-trial to come — making overall victory almost a formality — when he disappeared off the side of the Col de Perjuret in the Tarn gorges. He was found and brought back up to the road, but his broken back had ended his four years as a professional. Nencini won the Tour — the first Italian to do so since Fausto Coppi in 1952.

Anquetil was back in 1961, and for the next four years he was the toast of France, winning every time. In 1961 his

1961
1. Jacques Anquetil (F)
   122 hours 1 min 33 sec
2. Guido Carlesi (I)
   at 12 min 14 sec
3. Charly Gaul (Lux)
   at 12 min 16 sec
4. Imerio Massignan (I)
   at 15 min 59 sec
5. Hans Junkermann (WG)
   at 16 min 9 sec
6. Fernando Manzaneque (Sp)
   at 16 min 27 sec

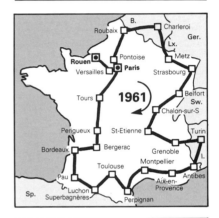

1962
1. Jacques Anquetil (F)
   114 hours 31 min 54 sec
2. Joseph Planckaert (B)
   at 4 min 59 sec
3. Raymond Poulidor (F)
   at 10 min 24 sec
4. Gilbert Desmet (B)
   at 13 min 1 sec
5. Ab Geldermans (Hol)
   at 14 min 4 sec
6. Tom Simpson (Eng)
   at 17 min 8 sec

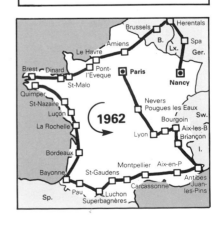

1963
1. Jacques Anquetil (F)
   113 hours 30 min 5 sec
2. Federico Bahamontes (Sp)
   at 3 min 35 sec
3. José Perez-Frances (Sp)
   at 10 min 14 sec
4. Jean-Claude Lebaube (F)
   at 11 min 55 sec
5. Gilbet Desmet (B)
   at 15 min 0 sec
6. Angelino Soler (Sp)
   at 15 min 4 sec

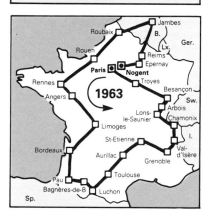

1964
1. Jacques Anquetil (F)
   127 hours 9 min 44 sec
2. Raymond Poulidor (F)
   at 55 sec
3. Federico Bahamontes (Sp)
   at 4 min 44 sec
4. Henri Anglade (F)
   at 5 min 42 sec
5. Georges Groussard (F)
   at 10 min 34 sec
6. André Foucher (F)
   at 10 min 36 sec

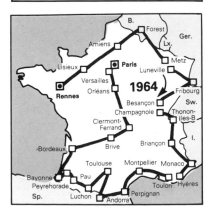

team-mate and friend André Darrigade won the opening stage (for the fifth time in six years!) but in the afternoon's 28.5-km time-trial Jacques took the lead, and never looked back all the way to Paris.

However, Anquetil was not gaining in popularity with the French spectators because his riding style was considered too clinical. He planned his route to victory with the perfection to be expected from this immaculately turned-out professional. He knew his own ability so well that he was able to perform whatever he had planned — and announced — thus taking away much of the interest in the race.

In 1962 Raymond Poulidor entered the arena, and Anquetil and Poulidor soon became the perfect double act. The crowds would boo Anquetil and cheer Poulidor, and both riders loved and reacted to this.

Despite the crowd's encouragement, the Limousin was not able to beat Anquetil (he finished third). Jacques won the race again, this time with a record average speed of 37.306 kph; he made his mark on the stony, unmade surfaces of the 9,200-ft climb of the Col de Restefond in the Alps. His victory was perhaps made a little easier by the loss of a number of strong riders, who gave up the struggle after they contracted food poisoning when they ate bad fish in the Pyrenees. Again, using the time-trial to his advantage, Anquetil won the 68-km test at Lyons to take the yellow jersey — with only two days to go to Paris.

Undoubtedly the greatest victory of the five came in 1963, when Anquetil took on the top climbers of the period and beat them at their own game. He won two major mountain stages in the Pyrenees at Bagnères-de-Bigorre, and later a stage in the Alps at Chamonix, where he took the lead. He was not just a time-triallist any longer.

Anquetil's last victory, in 1964, was especially sweet because a few weeks earlier he had won the Tour of Italy. Only Fausto Coppi had ever done the double in the same year (in fact, Coppi did it twice, in 1949 and 1952).

The Frenchman again took the overall lead after a time-trial, this time at Bayonne in the south-west, but not before Poulidor had forced him on to the defensive during a memorable stage in the mountains between Andorra and Toulouse.

Anquetil's Tour career ended on 11 July 1966, when he retired sick in a rain-storm. He stepped off his machine on the Côte de Serrières, near St Étienne; he would never again ride the race in which he had created history.

But he will always be remembered and in 1988, when the Tour passed the magnificent grave of Anquetil as it moved from Rouen to the day's start at Neufchâtel-en-Bray, many stopped to pay homage. The most famous riders, some carrying their own flowers, stood in silence to remember a unique man.

Eddy Merckx

Belgium had gone for more than twenty years without a win in the Tour de France, and the Belgians greeted the arrival of Eddy Merckx as their salvation.

Merckx soon became known as 'The Cannibal' because of his ruthless racing style, which always achieved the same result — victory. He was a born champion who won almost a third of the races in which he competed. One Dutch rider I spoke to at the 1975 Amstel Gold Classic in Holland summed up the feelings of many riders when he said, 'If Merckx has decided he wants to win today, then he will; otherwise it will be a very open race.' Merckx had decided he wanted to win.

Merckx was not popular with the French until his defeat in the Tour de France in 1975, for France, like many countries, seems to prefer champions to be beaten occasionally, and Merckx was just that bit too perfect! After his retirement he commented: 'I never tried to win the Tour more times than Anquetil, but when I entered the Tour I did so to win. It was the

> **Eddy Merckx — Career Record**
>
> *Name:* Eddy Merckx
> *Born:* Meensel-Kiezegem, 17.6.1945
> *Professional:* 1965–78
> *Principal Victories:*
> Five Tours de France. He competed seven times, winning 35 stages.
> Five Tours of Italy (1968, 1970, 1972, 1973, 1974). Won 25 stages.
> Tour of Switzerland (1974). Won five stages.
> Tour of Spain (1973). Won six stages.
> Tour of Belgium (1970, 1971). Won six stages.
> Paris–Nice (1969, 1970, 1971).
> World Road Champion (1967, 1971, 1974).
> World Hour Record holder (1972).
> Champion of Belgium (1970).
> The Classic single-day races.
> Paris–Roubaix (1968, 1970, 1973).
> Milan–San Remo (1966, 1967, 1969, 1971, 1972, 1975, 1976).
> Tour of Lombardy (1971, 1972).
> Liège–Bastogne–Liège (1969, 1971, 1972, 1973, 1975).
> Tour of Flanders (1969, 1975).
> Flèche–Wallonne (1967, 1970, 1972).
> Amstel Gold Race (1973, 1975).
> Merckx competed in 1,800 races, of which he won an amazing 525.

Eddy Merckx wore his world champion's rainbow jersey after losing his lead in the 1975 Tour after a crash. Here he struggles bravely to finish in second place. This performance made him more popular than when he won his five Tours.

Above: *One of the greatest dramas in Tour history was in 1971 when Luis Ocana was leading and all set to be the first rider to beat Eddy Merckx. He crashed on the descent of the Col de Mente.*

Below: *The last time Eddy Merckx wore the maillot jaune — his ninety-sixth! — was on the Col d'Altos in the Alps in 1975.*

most beautiful and most prestigious race in the world.' He rode the race seven times, winning five, and coming second and sixth in the other two.

Merckx began his 'term' in 1969 as a young 24-year-old, and although he had been the 1964 world amateur champion (when he was only nineteen), no one really expected him to become such a phenomenon.

The Tour began in Roubaix, a few kilometres from the Belgian frontier, and moved via Belgium in a clockwise direction around France to Paris. Once Merckx was on Belgian soil, he supplied the result his country had been waiting for, gaining his first yellow jersey after his Faema team won the team-time trial at Woluwe. During his career he was to wear the jersey on no fewer than ninety-six separate daily occasions, which is still the record today. But even while Jacques Goddet, the journalist and co-director of the Tour, was referring to him as 'Merckxissimo' in colourful articles in *L'Équipe*, other journalists were saying that Merckx was overdoing it, and would pay heavily in the Pyrenees.

They were soon to know better. Merckx did not defend his lead as the race swung south — some said it was because he thought the jersey would look nicer on his team-mate Julien Stevens, who became the leader for a while the very next day. After that, an individual display up the Ballon d'Alsace climb, the first mountain ever to be used in the Tour in 1905, was enough to get the lead back — and for good.

During the climb Merckx left behind some of the best riders of their time, beating among others the past Tour winners Felice Gimondi, Roger Pingeon and Jan Janssen, as well as the evergreen Raymond Poulidor, the affable ageing Frenchman. By the time the race finished in Paris, his margin over second-placed Pingeon was more than seventeen minutes. It was even worse for the Italian idol, Gimondi, as he was only fourth, and almost half an hour behind!

To crown his brilliant debut, Merckx won the last-stage time-trial of 36.8 km in Paris. The winner of the Tour really was the first man home.

Eddy was back again in

1970, and opened with a win in the Prologue time-trial at Limoges. (The Prologue time-trials were introduced to find a first leader for the race when it moved away from the start town on the first stage.) He was in tremendous form, having achieved a clutch of classic victories, including Paris–Roubaix, Flèche – Wallonne and Paris–Nice. He had also become the new Belgian champion, and was fresh from winning the 3,700-km Tour of Italy, so there was a chance to equal Coppi's and Anquetil's double. He lost his early lead to Italy's Italo Zilioli for a few days, but won it back at Valenciennes after crossing Northern France's famous cobblestones (known as the 'Hell of the North').

Merckx was a brilliant tactician, whose intelligent riding was always a pleasure to watch, even if it was sometimes too perfect to be compulsive viewing. Having regained the yellow jersey in the 1970 Tour, he was determined not to lose it again and he set about building his winning twelve-minute margin over his shadow, Joop Zoetemelk from Holland.

Eddy won the stage on the Ventoux, the first time the mountain had been included since the untimely death of Tom Simpson. A Catholic, he still found time to cross himself as he passed Simpson's memorial stone a kilometre from the finish that day. Although he won easily, gaining a record eight stage wins, he had noted two men to watch out for in the future, as their riding had impressed him during the race — Luis Ocana from Spain and Bernard Thevenet of France. He was right to remember them, as both would play a part in shaping his life in the Tour.

In 1971, the very next year, the talented Spanish climber Ocana dealt Eddy a blow that people were beginning to think was impossible when he won the stage from Grenoble to Orcières Merlette in the Alps, leaving Merckx almost ten minutes behind. But, only three days later Ocana was left lying among the gravel on a hairpin bend after crashing in a tremendous thunderstorm on the descent of the Col de Mente in the Pyrenees. His *maillot jaune* was covered in mud and torn

Merckx's Five Tour Results
1969
1. Eddy Merckx (B)
   116 hours 16 min 2 sec
2. Roger Pingeon (F)
   at 17 min 54 sec
3. Raymond Poulidor (F)
   at 22 min 13 sec
4. Felice Gimondi (I)
   at 29 min 24 sec
5. Andres Gandarias (Sp)
   at 33 min 4 sec
6. Rini Wagtmans (Hol)
   at 33 min 57 sec

1970
1. Eddy Merckx (B)
   at 119 hours 31 min 49 sec
2. Joop Zoetemelk (Hol)
   at 12 min 41 sec
3. Gosta Petterson
   (Sweden)
   at 15 min 54 sec
4. Martin Van Den Bossche (B)
   at 18 min 53 sec
5. Rini Wagtmans (Hol)
   at 19 min 54 sec
6. Lucien Van Impe (B)
   at 20 min 34 sec

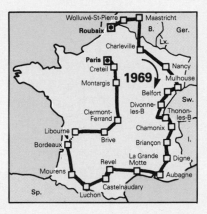

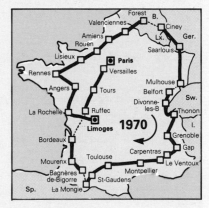

1971
1. Eddy Merckx (B)
   96 hours 45 min 14 sec
2. Joop Zoetemelk (Hol)
   at 9 min 51 sec
3. Lucien Van Impe (B)
   at 11 min 6 sec
4. Bernard Thevenet (F)
   at 14 min 50 sec
5. Joaquim Agostinho
   (Port)
   at 21 min 0 sec
6. Leif Mortensen (Dk)
   at 21 min 38 sec

1972
1. Eddy Merckx (B)
   108 hours 18 min 34 sec
2. Felice Gimondi (I)
   at 10 min 41 sec
3. Raymond Poulidor (F)
   at 11 min 34 sec
4. Lucien Van Impe (B)
   at 16 min 45 sec
5. Joop Zoetemelk (Hol)
   at 19 min 9 sec
6. Mariano Martinez (F)
   at 21 min 31 sec

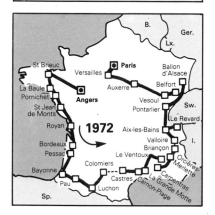

1974
1. Eddy Merckx (B)
   116 hours 53 min 3 sec
2. Raymond Poulidor (F)
   at 8 min 4 sec
3. Vincente Lopez-Carril
   (Sp)
   at 8 min 9 sec
4. Wladimiro Panizza (I)
   at 10 min 59 sec
5. Gonzalo Aja (Sp)
   at 11 min 24 sec
6. Joaquim Agostinho
   (Port)
   at 14 min 24 sec

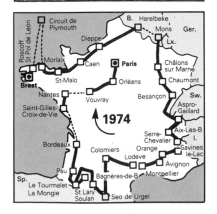

to pieces. Merckx was riding alongside Ocana when he fell, and by the end of the day had again taken the lead, while Ocana lay in hospital, fearing for his future as a racing cyclist. But two years later the Spaniard won his Tour de France.

In 1972 the route stayed in France throughout the race, and with the unbelievable Ocana back from his injuries, the obvious question was whether he could find again the form that had made Merckx look vulnerable in 1971.

The answer was no. Ocana tried to fight off bronchial pneumonia until finally the race doctors told him to give up, which he did at Aix-les-Bains.

Merckx won the Prologue at Angers, then lost his lead to Cyrille Guimard (the Frenchman who is now better known for having managed five winners of the Tour de France since his enforced retirement). Guimard's lead was only temporary, for he was not an outstanding climber, and after the crossing of the cols du Tourmalet, Aspin and Peyresourde in the Pyrenees it was business as usual, with Merckx back in yellow.

Besides Ocana, Merckx had listed Bernard Thevenet as a rival to be reckoned with, and the young Frenchman was progressing nicely. He had won the stage up Mont Ventoux, and this time he finished ninth overall.

Merckx decided to miss the 1973 Tour after having set the world hour record of 49.431 km in Mexico the previous October, having had his usual classic-winning spring and having won the Tour of Italy in June. The prospect of facing the toughest Tour route since the War and a back-to-form Luis Ocana did not appeal. (Ocana finally won his Tour.)

Eddy Merckx returned in 1974, the year the race made its historic visit to Britain when it arrived at Plymouth by boat and plane for the second stage. It was an unimaginative course up and down the Plympton by-pass, but it gave Britain a chance to glimpse this amazing athlete in action. The stage was won by Holland's Henk Poppe, with Merckx holding back until the mountains still some days away in far-off France.

In the days ahead, Raymond Poulidor, at thirty-eight, provided worthy opposition for Merckx, and on the 11-kilometre Pyrenean climb of the Plat d'Adet — a mountain standing at 5,000 feet and towering over the village of St Lary Soulan — the veteran Frenchman scored a win that pushed Merckx back into a mere fifth place on the stage, though he still kept his overall lead. There was another shock for Merckx when he lost a time-trial(!) beaten by Michel Pollentier, another Belgian, at Orléans. That defeat particularly annoyed Merckx, causing him to win the last stage into Paris to make his point. This was to be Eddy Merckx's last victory, for just like the ageing gunman, there's always someone coming along who is faster!

Bernard Thevenet won in 1975, the first time the race ended on the Champs Élysées. Merckx was second: his era was over.

Bernard Hinault

It took a little while, but sure enough, anything a Norman can do a Breton can do equally as well. The rivalry between the two *départements* of France has existed through history, and with the arrival of Bernard Hinault in 1978 it became clear that Jacques Anquetil could soon see his record equalled — or beaten — by another Frenchman.

Like Anquetil and Merckx, Hinault — a good-looking, proud man from the Brittany town of Yffiniac — had an air about him that singled him out from the rest.

Hinault's potential had already been realized by his manager Cyrille Guimard, another Breton, whose own promising career — which included yellow jerseys and seven stage wins in previous Tours de France — was ended by injury to his knees. Guimard was — and still is — a shrewd judge of athletes, and he made sure that Hinault did not ride in the Tour until he had developed his promise by becoming the first man since An-

Bernard Hinault — Career Record
Name: Bernard Hinault
Born: Yffiniac, 14.11.1954
Professional: 1974 (late) to 1986
Principal Victories:
Five Tours de France, competed eight times, winning 28 stages.
Tour of Italy (1980, 1982, 1985).
Tour of Spain (1978, 1983).
Tour of Luxembourg (1982).
World Champion (1980).
French Champion (1978).
Paris–Roubaix (1981).
Tour of Lombardy (1979, 1984).
Liège–Bastogne–Liège (1977, 1980).
Fleche–Wallonne (1977, 1983).
Amstel Gold Race (1981).

Bernard Hinault, good-looking and ambitious, always rode to win in his eight Tours. The Frenchman won five of his Tours and finished second twice. He retired injured when leading in the eighth.

quetil to win the single-day classic races for France. When Hinault arrived in Leiden, Holland, for the 1978 Tour he had already gained the distinction of being the first man since Anquetil to win the Liège–Bastogne–Liège and Ghent–Wevelgem classics. He had put an end to twelve years of French famine with these two famous Belgian races, and he was now ready for the Big One.

Like Anquetil and Merckx, Hinault was an excellent time-triallist, virtually unbeatable in races alone against the watch. Anquetil's nickname had been 'Maître'; and Merckx's 'The Cannibal'; before long the Press, riders and officials had also found a name for Bernard, calling him, 'Le Blaireau' — The Badger. The badger is a quiet, peace-loving animal, an animal which if forced into a corner fights its way out. This described Hinault well.

This was the typical scene that greeted Bernard Hinault every time he finished a stage. Perhaps this explains his tendency to hit out at the Press.

It was Hinault, then the French road champion, who led the riders walking over the finish line at Valence d'Agen, complaining about the long stages and lack of rest. He has lashed out several times: another occasion on which he revealed his quick temper was during the Paris–Nice stage race, when, after being forced to stop by demonstrators blocking the road he landed a blow on one of them of which any practised boxer would have been proud. A professional rider who witnessed the incident said 'Bernard saw the crowd blocking the road and just put his head down and raced straight for them. He was so annoyed when he was stopped that he just got off his bike and started hitting out.'

At stage finishes of the Tour de France Hinault has often displayed his frustration at being crowded into a corner by photographers and journalists who should have known better. He even won the Paris–Roubaix classic in 1981 so that he could tell the organizers why he would never ride such a race again!

It did not take followers of the Tour long to realize that Hinault was no ordinary man, and if nothing else, that he was certainly in charge of his own destiny!

Hinault retired on 14 November (his thirty-second birthday), as he always said he would, and he since has joined the Société du Tour de France on a part-time basis, as a technical adviser.

Bernard Hinault was a single-minded person who like Anquetil and Merckx demanded perfection, so, when he started his first race around France, few felt he would lose.

The 23-year-old had chosen the 65th anniversary of the Tour for his debut, but little was seen of him as the race wound its way from The Hague, through the Paris suburbs and on towards Bordeaux. He pounced on the eighth day with a 27.5 mph win in the 59-km time-trial at Ste Foy la Grande, and although he did not gain enough time to take the lead, he reminded everyone he was ready for the nine mountainous days to come.

The race had been led for a long time by two Belgians, Joseph Bruyère and the sprinter Freddy Maertens, who in 1976 had matched Merckx's record of eight stage wins. However, by the rest day at Biarritz and with the Pyrenees ahead, Bruyère was expected to lose his lead, and Hinault hoped he would move up from fifth place overall.

By the time the giant peaks of the Pyrenees had been climbed and there had been the walk by the striking riders at Valence d'Agen, Hinault had improved to second overall. He was not unhappy with such a position at this stage of the race with the Alps still to come, although he was perhaps surprised that Bruyère was still in yellow. At Alpe d'Huez Belgian

The whole race protested against the long days of the 1978 Tour by walking over the finish line at Valence d'Agen. Bernard Hinault (hand behind back) was the spokesman. The Fiat rider (left) is Paul Sherwen from Cheshire in his first of seven Tours. Others in the front row are: Gerben Karstens (TI-Raleigh), Michel Pollentier (King of the Mountains leader), Hinault (in French champion's jersey), Freddy Maertens (points leader) and Jan Raas (TI-Raleigh).

Bernard Hinault was one of the best time-trial riders ever to compete in the Tour de France. In 1981 he was the first rider to beat 51 kph for an individual test.

champion Michel Pollentier made a piece of unwelcome Tour history when he was disqualified after he was found with a device fitted about his body with the intention of cheating the dope control. Pollentier — who had taken the lead off Bruyère — became the first to be disqualified for such a reason. The lead passed to the second man, who was now Joop Zoetemelk from Holland. As he was to prove in his later Tours, Hinault knew his capabilities well, and, with a long time-trial to end this race at Metz, he was always confident of winning.

After the Alps, and with the loss of Raleigh's Dutch hope Hennie Kuiper after he struck an overhanging rock with his head, the race became a battle between Zoetemelk and Hinault. No one doubted that the latter would win in the end, which he did by almost four minutes. He had also achieved something tht had eluded Anquetil — he had won the race as the reigning French champion. Anquetil, incredibly, never won the home title.

The following year Hinault was back for a race route of 'only' 3,700 km which included four individual time trials and, above all a stage into his home town (almost) of St Brieuc in Brittany. He made a spectacular start by winning the first time-trial up the steep and twisting mountain of Superbagnères above Luchon in the Pyrenees, arriving home in the leader's yellow jersey.

What a welcome! There were 300,000 people chanting his name and waving placards. The Prodigal Son really had come home, if only for a night.

After this, with the home pressures of leading through Brittany relieved, Hinault let his lead slip as the race swung away to Belgium. Evergreen Joop Zoetemelk took over, but there was plenty of time yet. Choosing the mountain time-trial — this year at the ski station at Avoriaz in the Alps — Hinault won and Zoetemelk was second. Tour number two was in the bag.

The following year, in 1980, Hinault became the ninth rider to retire while wearing the leader's yellow jersey, but unlike Pollentier, he was not in any disgrace. Hinault pulled out at Pau, announcing his departure from the Tour at 10 p.m. in the evening, which was too late for most newspapers to carry the story. He had been suffering from a knee strain that was only to be cured by surgery later. The obvious question at the time was: 'Were two Tours his limit?'

Hinault was back in 1981 with a scar on his knee which marked a successful operation. He was as determined as ever. The race started in Nice, and he opened in the yellow jersey after the six-kilometre Prologue time-trial along the famous Promenade des Anglais. He had set the amazing time of 6 minutes 48 seconds, an average speed of 32 mph! All it seemed he had to prove now was that he could still climb hills.

The Badger did not defend his lead immediately, but within a week he had it back for the rest of the Tour. The wheel had turned a full circle in almost exactly a year as Hinault pulled on the yellow jersey at Pau, the same place where he had walked out of the race in 1980.

Hinault always had a leaning to the theatrical and all that remained for him was to build his lead all the way to Paris, which he did, winning by over 14 minutes — the biggest margin of his three wins. He had now equalled Louison Bobet's hat-trick, which put him on the same level as another famous Breton. Hinault's fourth win was to come in 1982, his fifth attempt at the race. This time the route started in Switzerland, a country that had not won the race since Hugo Koblet's victory in 1951.

The route was said to favour Hinault because of the long time-trials, and the experts were proved right as the race left Basle and headed north towards Belgium before making enormous transfers by train and plane to start again in France. Hinault won the Prologue but lost his lead next day to Ludo Peeters from Belgium. It stayed that way until the race arrived at Valence d'Agen, the town in Gascony where Hinault had led the race over the line *à pied*.

This time it was different, Hinault had the chance to turn on the style in a 57-km time-trial, but it did not work out as you might expect. Bernard Hinault did not win. He was beaten by former world champion Dutchman Gerrie Knetemann, who said, 'I once beat Hinault in a Prologue time-trial in 1979, but I don't count that; it's not a real time trial like this one. I still can't believe it.' Knetemann, a most humorous character, beat Hinault by just 18 seconds, but Hinault on Bastille Day was the new leader, in front again and never to be headed all the way to Paris. Like Merckx, he would never admit to chasing membership of the exclusive '5' club, but after his win in 1982 the thought must have crossed his mind!

However, fate struck in 1983 and Hinault withdrew injured, leaving the way clear for Laurent Fignon to become the first Parisian to win the race in Paris. Almost overnight Hinault had competition, and like Anquetil, it was coming from his own country. What was worse, it was coming from within his own Renault team, as Fignon had been discovered by Cyrille Guimard, Hinault's manager. There was also a third name to consider — the American Greg LeMond, who had never ridden a Tour de France, but encouraged by both Hinault and Guimard was showing all the signs of a champion. In 1984 it was to be the big showdown, for all three were riding the Tour. However, Hinault had left Guimard's side less than amicably, after disagreeing about who should be in charge of the Renault team — himself or Fignon. For the time being LeMond stayed with Fignon and Guimard.

But Hinault on Bastille Day was the new leader.

Hinault's Five Tour Results
1978
1. Bernard Hinault (F)
   108 hours 18 min 0 sec
2. Joop Zoetemelk (Hol)
   at 3 min 56 sec
3. Joaquim Agostinho (Port)
   at 6 min 54 sec
4. Joseph Bruyère (B)
   at 9 min 4 sec
5. Christian Seznec (F)
   at 12 min 50 sec
6. Paul Wellens (B)
   at 14 min 38 sec

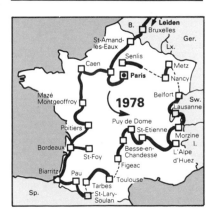

Bernard Hinault ended the fourteenth stage of the 1985 Tour de France at St Étienne with a broken nose. Hinault crashed yards from the finish line, and in order to continue next day he had to remount and cross the line despite his injuries.

Hinault went to La Vie Claire, a team created for him by entrepreneur Bernard Tapis, and he finished second behind Fignon, with LeMond third.

After Fignon's two years on top, 1985 rung the changes on him as he was sidelined with a leg injury not dissimilar to that suffered by Hinault in 1980, while LeMond — who was also nursing thoughts of one day winning the Tour — had left Fignon's Renault team to join Hinault's La Vie Claire squad.

The race started in Brittany, and predictably Hinault snatched all the early publicity, not least because he arrived at the Plumelec start by bike! He won the Prologue time-trial again, and at first it looked as though he was his old self. He played one of his aces at Strasbourg, winning the 75-km time-trial to take the lead, but as the race progressed it began to look as though he wouldn't make it.

LeMond (who had lost over two minutes in the time-trial to Hinault) was lying second overall, 2 minutes 32 seconds behind the Frenchman. After the climb to Avoriaz on the eleventh stage (won by Colombia's Luis Herrera) LeMond finished second on the stage, but exactly four minutes behind. This was a lot of time to lose, and it seemed a pyrrhic victory, for Hinault was coming up.

Then at St Étienne, and with the Pyrenees still to come, disaster struck when Hinault crashed in the sprint finish, landing heavily on his face. Covered in blood, which was dripping on to his crossbar, he remounted and wobbled to the finish line. He immediately blamed the Australian Phil Anderson for the accident. Anderson, however, angrily refused to be made the scapegoat.

Because of a rule in stage racing which says that if you crash inside the last kilometre (providing you cross the line later) you will be given the same time as the group you were with when you crashed, Hinault kept his yellow jersey. A matter of more concern to him was whether he would be able to race again next day, for he had a broken nose and a bruised body.

Hinault met his anxious family at the entrance to his hotel, not far from the finishing line on the Cours Fauriel. With his injuries, he looked as if he had met up with Mohammed Ali in his heyday. His young son Michael burst out crying, and Hinault bent down, put his nose to Michael's face and said: 'Touch my nose — I'm O.K. You see, there's nothing wrong. It's all over.' As he walked into the hotel, those watching knew he would be back for the next day's 237-km fifteenth stage to Aurillac. He continued with a large black eye, cheered on as a hero.

Hinault had won his personal fight against his injury, but there was still one threat to his fifth victory — his team-mate Greg LeMond, still in second place overall.

LeMond was riding to the unwritten law that you never attack a team-mate, especially when he is ahead of you on the overall classification, yet he found himself presented with the opportunity to become the first ever American to win the Tour. It happened in the Pyrenees when Irishman Stephen Roche, lying third overall, attacked during the 209-km seventeenth stage from Toulouse to Luz Ardiden, and LeMond was quick to follow the move. Hinault was left struggling in the group behind. Roche urged LeMond on, telling him he could become the first American winner, while the Irishman himself finished second overall. The pair gained time on the finishing climb.

During the ascent Paul Koichli, the La Vie Claire team's Swiss manager, came alongside LeMond in his car and a heated discussion took place as the American protested at being unable to win the Tour for himself.

1979
1. Bernard Hinault (F)
   103 hours 6 min 50 sec
2. Joop Zoetemlek (Hol)
   at 13 min 37 sec
3. Joaquim Agostinho (Port)
   at 26 min 53 sec
4. Hennie Kuiper (Hol)
   at 28 min 2 sec
5. Jean-René Bernaudeau
   at 32 min 43 sec
6. Giovanni Battaglin (I)
   at 38 min 12 sec

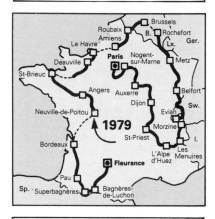

1981
1. Bernard Hinault (F)
   96 hours 19 min 38 sec
2. Lucien Van Impe (B)
   at 14 min 34 sec
3. Robert Alban (F)
   at 17 min 4 sec
4. Joop Zoetemelk (Hol)
   at 18 min 21 sec
5. Peter Winnen (Hol)
   at 20 min 26 sec
6. Jean-René Bernaudeau (F)
   at 23 min 2 sec

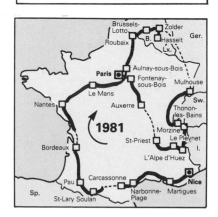

1982
1. Bernard Hinault (F)
   92 hours 8 min 46 sec
2. Joop Zoetemelk (Hol)
   at 6 min 21 sec
3. Johan Van Der Velde
   (Hol)
   at 8 min 59 sec
4. Peter Winnen (Hol)
   at 9 min 24 sec
5. Phil Anderson (Aust)
   at 12 min 16 sec
6. Beat Breu (Switz)
   at 13 min 21 sec

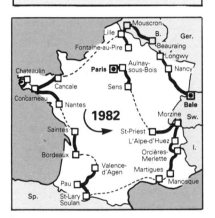

1985
1. Bernard Hinault (F)
   113 hours 24 min 23 sec
2. Greg LeMond (USA)
   at 1 min 42 sec
3. Stephen Roche (Ire)
   at 4 min 29 sec
4. Sean Kelly (Ire)
   at 6 min 26 sec
5. Phil Anderson (Aust)
   at 7 min 44 sec
6. Pedro Delgado (Sp)
   at 11 min 53 sec

Hinault finished exhausted in eighteenth place, losing over a minute to the American, and the friendship that had been evident between the two riders would never be quite the same again. Hinault went on to win his fifth Tour, but LeMond continued to cause him concern as he nibbled away at his overall lead, even winning the 45-km time-trial in the Limousin. Here LeMond beat Hinault by five seconds, another reason to feel that the young American had all the qualities to win the Tour soon.

However, this time Hinault was the winner in Paris; equalling the record of Anquetil and Merckx, although in 1986 LeMond would be in no mood to take second place again.

Chapter 4
The Great Losers

Raymond Poulidor, whose face became known throughout Europe during fourteen Tours de France.

Raymond Poulidor — career record
Name: Raymond Poulidor
Born: Masbaraud-
  Merignat, 15.4.1936
Professional: 1960–77
Principal Placings:
Tour de France — 2nd in
  1964, 1965, 1974; 3rd in
  1962, 1966, 1969, 1972,
  1976; Seven stage wins in
  14 Tours.
Tour of Spain — 1st 1964
  and 2nd 1965.
Paris–Nice — 1st 1971,
  1972; 2nd 1972, 1973.
Classics:
Paris–Tours — 2nd 1976;
  3rd 1963.
Milan–San Remo — 1st
  1961; 2nd 1964.
Tour of Lombardy — 3rd
  1966, 1967.
Liège–Bastogne–Liège —
  3rd 1968.
Fleche–Wallonne — 1st
  1963; 2nd 1972.
GP des Nations — 1st
  1963; 2nd 1969; 3rd
  1965.
World Road Championship
  — 2nd 1974; 3rd 1961,
  1964, 1966.
French Champion — 1961;
  2nd 1965.

Raymond Poulidor

Raymond Poulidor gave the French public a choice — they could cheer the winner or they could cheer him. Almost without exception, they chose to cheer Poulidor, the loser who never failed to win their hearts.

Despite his fourteen attempts, 'Pou-pou' never won the Tour de France. Even worse, he never even put on the race leader's yellow jersey, even for a day. Yet he was undoubtedly the most popular rider of his time.

His sharp features — pointed nose, projecting chin and impish smile — were a cartoonist's delight, and the amazing courage he showed in his constant refusal to give up the battle won him a following of doting fans. One sometimes wonders how they would have felt if he had ever converted one of his eight places in the first three in the Tour into an actual win. At thirty-eight (an age when most riders have hung up their wheels three or four years previously) Poulidor finished second in the Tour de France, and recognizing this magnificent achievement, winner Eddy Merckx held the arms of his runner-up aloft in Paris. At forty, before he finally retired, Poulidor would be on the podium again, this time having finished third.

Poulidor lived through one of the most competitive periods of the Tour de France. His career began during the Anquetil era and ended only a year before Merckx himself retired, giving him an amazing seventeen years as a professional.

Poulidor had none of the consistency of his two most feared adversaries, for although he was more gifted than most, he did not have the make-up of the complete champion. But he could certainly turn in a fast time-trial and could climb mountains, as he proved on several memorable occasions, beating Anquetil in a time-trial and bettering Merckx on La Turbie climb in Paris–Nice in 1972 and 1973. He could also win in the sprint, and finish ahead of the field alone in the road-race stages — and yet he still lacked the ability to make the right decisions during the racing itself. As a result, he never became a Tour winner.

Poulidor conjured up the image of a pop star — with the roadsides of Europe as his stage. I remember watching him arrive in a village square in 1976. He often left his appearance in the stage-start arena until late, but you always knew when he had arrived — he was forced to run the gauntlet along a corridor of noise, with the crowd chanting 'Pou-pou, Pou-pou!'

Poulidor always totally ignored his following. Once I saw him sitting down on a park-type bench, peeling an orange and pushing it into his back pocket, while behind him old ladies of seventy reached forward, wishing their arms were three inches longer, so that they could touch the biggest loser of them all!

The eternal second (as he eventually became known) lost one Tour by only 55 seconds to Anquetil, and this was the one he really should have won. There was a time bonus of a minute offered to the stage winner at Monaco. Poulidor sprinted a lap too soon on the velodrome and lost out — Anquetil did not make such a mistake! In another two races, in 1968 and 1973, he was forced to withdraw after an accident, but everyone knew he would be back.

Two nations in particular appreciated Poulidor's great spirit: Belgium awarded him the Order of Leopold II in 1975 and France gave him her honour of Chevalier of the Legion of Honour in 1972. As the years passed it became apparent that the cyclist — who by the way was (and still is) a great poker-player — was never going to win the Tour, and this endeared him even more to the French people.

Poulidor grew up in a cycling family, although his brothers, Henri and André, raced only as amateurs. Limoges — and Creuse in particular, where the Poulidors grew up — is marvellous country for the cyclist, with its beautiful wooded river

Raymond Poulidor rode fourteen Tours, but one of his finest was against the great Eddy Merckx (pictured in the yellow jersey). Poulidor, when thirty-eight, finished second to Merckx.

The eternal second lost one tour to Anquetil by only 55 seconds.

valleys and plateaux, which are never higher than 3,500 feet above sea level.

Poulidor's first Tour was in 1962. This was when Anquetil had already won twice and was looking for victory number three. However, Poulidor was spared the embarrassment of having to ride in the same French national team as Anquetil because the Tour had reverted to trade teams. Anquetil rode for St Raphaël, a drinks firm, while Poulidor represented Mercier–BP, a joint sponsorship between a French bicycle-builder and the petroleum company. He won the spectators' hearts right from this very first Tour because he started with a broken wrist, wearing a specially designed cast.

Despite this handicap, Poulidor not only won the stage between Aix-les-Bains and Briançon, but finished third in the following day's time-trial to Lyons, beaten only by Anquetil and the great Italian Ercole Baldini. Third place overall was quite a debut. Poulidor was already twenty-eight by his second Tour in 1964, having spent two years in army service in Africa. This was to be a marvellous duel in true French tradition. It was arguably the most exciting of the fifty-one races so far, and in the end Poulidor lost to Anquetil by only 55 seconds — then the smallest margin in history. Earlier in this chapter I mentioned how Poulidor messed up the finish on the track in Monaco where Anquetil took a minute's bonus and Britain's Tom Simpson came a notable second. But during the race rest-day in Andorra, Anquetil had seen a fortune-teller and was told that he would not finish the race. And indeed — perhaps with the fortune-teller's predictions in mind — he fell back on the next day's stage up the Col d'Envalira, losing over four minutes to the leaders, including Poulidor.

After a great deal of persuasion, Anquetil continued, and by the end of the day he was back in the race and still a challenger. He had chased the leaders hard, and, as so often happens, Lady Luck switched sides. Poulidor, the man with most to gain from Anquetil's difficulties, buckled a wheel and was forced to stop thirteen miles from the stage finish. A routine change became a nightmare when his over-enthusiastic mechanic pushed him off his bike as he tried to help him back into the fray.

Anquetil, although still not leading the Tour itself, finished almost three minutes ahead of Poulidor. The next day Poulidor countered with another attack in the Pyrenees at Luchon, regaining practically all the time he had lost to his rival. With the Puy de Dôme mountain above Clermont-Ferrand still to come, he was back in with a chance.

This famous French beauty spot was to provide the platform for the great showdown, and as if joined together they climbed the helter-skelter road around the mountain side by side. Poulidor forced the pace, giving Anquetil the most painful

Missing the yellow jersey by just 15 seconds!

period of his career, but the Norman would not give in. He knew that if he could defend himself successfully here the pendulum would swing in his favour in the time-trial to follow.

Poulidor managed to shake Anquetil off towards the end of the climb, but unfortunately the two brilliant Spanish climbers Julio Jimenez and Federico Bahamontes were ahead to take the finishing-time bonuses that could have changed the destiny of the race. Poulidor was third, gaining 42 seconds on Anquetil and missing the yellow jersey by just 15 seconds! And Anquetil, having suffered to save the leadership, was in no mood for losing in the time-trial at Versailles two days later. Poulidor had had his chance and muffed it, and Anquetil went on to win by less than a minute. In 1965 Anquetil was replaced by a new professional — the Italian Felice Gimondi — and Poulidor came second again. 'It's no good,' said Raymond in Paris, 'I have no complaints, Gimondi was the best.' Nevertheless, journalists and public alike remained convinced that it would only be a matter of time before Poulidor won a Tour de France, and the 1967 race looked set to be the one.

After the opening time-trial at Angers the Press rushed to the telephone, not to file their stories, but to ring Poulidor's hotel and congratulate him on his first yellow jersey! They, like everyone else, had thought that the opening 5.8-km time-trial had been won by the Frenchman. But shortly afterwards it was announced that the Spaniard José-Maria Errandonea had won by a scant fifth of a second!

Thirteen teams took part in a race which saw the return to the national formula rather than the trade team make-up. This meant that Poulidor, a trade-team rival of last year's winner Lucien Aimar, was now in the same French national team, along with his own season-long Mercier-BP team-mate Roger Pingeon. All three were declared 'protected' riders by the manager, 65-year-old Marcel Bidot. Poulidor, the team leader, was once again the favourite, until fate changed the Tour pattern. In the Vosges mountains he was not paying attention — or was it another indication of his lack of intelligent race reading? — and he missed a strong attack by many of the favoured riders, including Britain's Tom Simpson, Aimar, Pingeon, Felice Gimondi (the winner in 1965) and Jan Janssen. He realized his error, and was pursuing in a desperate attempt to recover from the surprise move. It should have been a routine attack and counter-attack, but it was not. Up front Gimondi punctured, and Janssen (who was to win the Tour of 1968) attacked violently in an attempt to leave Gimondi. The Italian never rejoined.

The increase in pace up ahead had put Poulidor in terrible trouble, and to make matters worse, he punctured and crashed down a mountain just before the finishing climb up the Ballon d'Alsace. Although uninjured he had wrecked his bike, so with no team car near him, he stopped Edouard Delberghe, a team-mate, and took his!

Poulidor was panicked into a violent chase on a machine which was not quite the same size as his own, and on the climb of the Ballon his strength and morale left him. He lost an enormous 12 minutes — and the race. At the finish Pingeon had taken the lead and, as a protected rider, could claim help from the rest of his team. Poulidor, also a protected rider, could no longer expect his team to work for him when another team member was in a far stronger position to win. But the question of loyalties never arose and Poulidor became Pingeon's *domestique extraordinaire*!

Of course, if Poulidor had been the mercenary Anquetil, Pingeon would never have slept so easily in his bed at night, because Anquetil would have fought to get back his lost time in the Alps and Pyrenees and the time-trials still to come.

A few days later Pingeon was in terrible difficulty on the Col de Galibier. Ahead of him was Gimondi, looking to regain lost time, and the great Spanish climber Julio Jiminez, hoping to take the yellow jersey into Spain, where the race was still to go. Everyone, even the leader, usually experiences one bad day in a Tour, and the Alps was certainly the one for Pingeon. He fell back with the faithful Poulidor coaxing him, pacing him and all but dragging him to the summit of the Galibier.

Raymond Poulidor, his chances already gone in 1967, became the perfect team-mate to Roger Pingeon. Poulidor rode by his side on the Puy de Dôme, encouraging him to keep going when the race got tough. Pingeon won the race, and Poulidor was the first to congratulate him.

The question everyone was asking was 'Why doesn't Pouli-dor go ahead and win the stage, so that later he may be in a position to win the race?' Poulidor, though, was a man of honour: Pingeon was a team-mate who had not yet lost the race, and Poulidor was in a position to help. The late Jock Wadley, a British journalist who followed twenty-two Tours de France, witnessed this show of defiance and commented at the time: 'I am convinced that if Poulidor had not nursed the ailing Pingeon so tenderly, then he would have lost his yellow jersey.'

Poulidor's assistance was not to be restricted to the Galibier. Poulidor was alongside Pingeon on the Ventoux, the Tourmalet and the Puy de Dôme. The only time he left Pingeon's side was to counter a move by Jimenez, and he punctured again, to finish only eighth in Luchon!

Pingeon finally won the race by 3 minutes 40 seconds, with the aggressive balding Spanish climber Jimenez coming second. The scenes at the finish were remarkable — even for the Tour de France! Those with long memories perhaps recalled the 1930 Tour, the first time national teams had been created, when Charles Pélissier had helped team-mate André Leducq win in similar fashion. In Paris the cheers were for both men, as Poulidor hugged and kissed Pingeon with such obvious sincerity. Again he had been a truly marvellous loser.

In 1974 Poulidor was thirty-eight, and had gained four third places in a period of nine years. He was surely out of the running. He was not! Poulidor had finished second when Anquetil had won his fifth race in 1964; the 1974 Tour was to be a repeat performance, with Merckx winning his fifth Tour and Poulidor again coming second. Merckx, being Merckx, won by an enormous eight minutes, which hardly made this a vintage race. Poulidor, though, was by this time almost a veteran, and now instead of being called the 'eternal second', he had been renamed 'young eternal second'!

During fourteen Tours de France, Raymond Poulidor was the actor who drew most of the applause without playing the lead role. His attacking riding — coupled with his bad luck or bad judgment — made this period one of the most interesting in the Tour's history. Only very occasionally does Poulidor pay the race a visit these days. Instead he has returned to the quiet life around Limoges; his days of being every French youngster's hero are but a memory.

But he can look back at his record eight places in the top three in the Tour de France and take consolation in the fact that, if he had worn the yellow jersey after the opening time-trial in Angers in 1967, his folklore image would have been spoilt!

Joop Zoetemelk

Joop Zoetemelk always wanted to be a cyclist. Even after retiring at the end of last season, he has continued riding for enjoyment and remained part of the Tour circus (as a public relations man with the Super Confex company, with whom he rode out his last season).

Unlike Poulidor, Zoetemelk did win one Tour (in 1980), but he was always criticized for his negative riding style. He was accused of riding the race, not to win, but merely to profit by the mistakes of others.

'Joopy' earned two unflattering nicknames — 'The Rat' and 'The Sucker', because he was said to follow in the slipstream of others — though he deserved neither. But when his career ended after an all-time record of sixteen completed Tours de France he was as loved and admired as any of those who had gone before.

Only age forced Zoetemelk to retire. If his body could have kept up, then he would never have stopped leading the life to which he had become addicted. Like Poulidor, he had crossed the paths of the Tour Greats, but whereas Poulidor got Anquetil and Merckx, Zoetemelk was landed with Merckx and with France s new ace Bernard Hinault.

> **Joop Zoetemelk – Career Record**
> *Name:* Joop Zoetemelk
> *Born:* The Hague, 2.12.1946
> *Professional:* 1970–87
> *Principal Placings:*
> Tour de France — 1st in 1980; 2nd in 1970, 1971, 1976, 1978, 1979, 1982; 3rd none; 4th in 1973, 1975, 1981; 10 stage wins.
> Tour of Spain — 1st 1979.
> Tour of Holland — 1st in 1975.
> Paris–Nice — 1974, 1975, 1979.
> *Classics:*
> Amstel Gold Race — 1987.
> Paris–Tours — 1977.
> Blois–Chaville — 1979.
> Fleche-Wallonne — 1976.
> World Road Championship — 1985.
> Dutch champion — 1971, 1973.

Joop Zoetemelk retired in 1987, having been Holland's outstanding rider for almost twenty years, but in the Tour de France he will always be remembered as the man who nearly made it.

The baby-faced Dutchman was a man of character and courage. He had his ambitions, and despite his advancing years, he was always ready to turn a race situation in his favour if the opportunity arose. Just when it seemed he was never going to win the Tour, at thirty-three years old, Zoetemelk finally won his yellow jersey when Bernard Hinault abandoned at Pau.

The Dutchman's twilight years were among his most memorable, and not least the happy moment when at thirty-eight he broke clear of a group of riders in the last mile to win his only world road-racing title in Italy. In 1987, at the veteran age of forty, he was selected for the world championship again, but the Union Cycliste Internationale invoked the rule that said a veteran rider could not be selected. The Dutch Cycling Federation appealed against this because of Zoetemelk's exceptional ability, and he was allowed to take part. The rule was changed in 1988. In addition to the world championship, Zoetemelk also became the oldest man to win the Amstel Gold Race classic last season in his own country. A perfect way to end a marvellously competitive career.

All this might never have happened, for Zoetemelk was involved in a serious crash in 1974 which left him fighting for his life. Even when he recovered, the doctors considered his career as a top cyclist almost certainly over.

Zoetemelk made his entry on to the professional scene in 1970, after having already achieved success as an amateur, winning a gold medal in the 100-km team time-trial in the 1968 Olympic Games in Mexico and gaining a reputation as a noted stage-race rider in the amateur Tours.

This was the Tour that Zoetemelk felt would never come — the one he won! In 1980 the Dutchman wore the maillot jaune *for the last ten days. In front here is Lucien Van Impe, who beat Zoetemelk in 1976.*

His victory in the Tour de l'Avenir (literally, Tour of the Future) — then seen as the amateur version of the Tour de France — had also brought him to the public's attention. Zoetemelk had led from the fourth stage until the finish in Paris, and had also been the best climber in the Tour of Austria and winner of the Tour of Yugoslavia. The professional ranks beckoned.

When Zoetemelk did turn professional he had little chance against Merckx. He lost both the 1970 and 1971 Tours by several minutes, but despite the margin he did finish second each time, which made him a hot favourite for the future.

Although Zoetemelk always had expected to lose these Tours, he blamed his manager, Brik Schotte, for the size of the losing margins. 'I was made to work too hard to help the De Vlaeminck brothers to win stages,' he complained. In 1974, therefore, he left the Belgian Flandria team and joined Raymond Poulidor's GAN–Mercier team, the team with the famous mauve colours.

Zoetemelk has always been a Francophile. He married a French girl, Françoise, and unlike most Dutchmen, he speaks French as his second language and has no English. With Poulidor and the new manager, the respected Louis Caput, Zoetemelk hoped for better things. He had a spectacular start to his 1974 season.

The Paris–Nice race in March is almost as renowned as the Tour itself and used to take place over ten days. It is a favourite with the top riders, being one of the earliest clashes of the new season, and also has a great following in the Press. It was an early opportunity for Zoetemelk to show himself off against Merckx. Zoetemelk had been known to answer the critics who said he always rode in Merckx's shadow by saying that that was in itself a considerable feat. After he had won the Paris–Nice race (his first of three victories) by beating Merckx on the Col d'Eze mountain above Nice, it was Merckx's turn to comment: 'It was the first time I had doubted myself,' he said, 'but I refused to accept that Joop would be my superior.' But he was; Merckx finished third overall, and the Mercier team — and 'Petit' Louis Caput in particular — now awaited the Tour de France with bated breath.

How cruel life can be.

The accident happened in the Midi–Libre stage race in the May of 1974, as Zoetemelk was building up for a serious attempt at the Tour. Just as he came around a corner at full speed an English-registered car wandered on to the closed-road finishing circuit, and a collision was inevitable. Zoetemelk was first taken to his hotel and then rushed to hospital in Béziers. From there he was transferred to Meaux, where his wife was waiting. The doctors told him that if he had been flown in instead of coming by car, the pressure change would have killed him. He was a lucky man.

Holland has produced a few top challengers for the Tour. Here Joop Zoelemelk (right) and Hennie Kuiper are both under pressure in the mountains in 1978. Bernard Hinault, the final winner, concentrates behind.

Raymond Martin (left) Zoetemelk, Van Impe, Robert Alban and Bernard Thevenet set the pace in the Alps in 1980. Martin won his only Mountains title, and Zoetemelk won his only Tour.

So, instead of riding the tour he had anticipated so eagerly, Zoetemelk began his eight months' road to recovery. That is a long time, especially when the average career span of a professional cyclist is said to be only eight years. Zoetemelk and Poulidor were clearly not in the sample taken to arrive at such a figure. Zoetemelk's body and fractured skull mended gradually and by the time the Tour ended on the Parc des Princes (the last time the Tour ended here) the Dutchman was well enough to take a lap of honour, saying he would be back in 1975.

The doctors predicted that he would not recover all his original talents on a bike, but they should have been in Nice in March 1975 when Zoetemelk defended his title. As my Irish journalist friends would say: 'And, your man Merckx was only second!'

Yes, Joopy was well on the road to full recovery.

The summer Tour, the first to end on the Champs-Élysées, became a battle between Merckx and Thevenet, with Zoetemelk finishing a magnificent fourth, the winner of two stages. He won many smaller races, but he was a man for the Tour de France, and this was always his target each season. In 1976, after Merckx decided not to ride, Zoetemelk felt he had a chance of victory — but he made the mistake of ignoring a little Belgian climber.

Lucien Van Impe had already won the King of the Mountains title three times, and at thirty he felt it was just possible he could continue long enough to beat Federico Bahamontes's record of six wins. Age was against him, though: if he was ever going to win the Tour outright he had to make his bid soon, and this was the year he had decided upon.

Van Impe, who had attacked 70 km earlier, won in the Pyrenees on the 5,000-ft Pla d'Adet climb which ended the stage from St Gaudens, a stage that counted heavily towards the title King of the Mountains. This time it also gave Van Impe the race lead, paving the way to his only victory in fifteen Tours. (He did, incidentally, equal Bahamontes's climbing record in 1983, though he never beat it.)

Zoetemelk had again paid heavily. He had paid close attention to the riders he thought could win the Tour — the previous year's winner, Bernard Thevenet, and the race leader Raymond Delisle — but had dismissed Van Impe as a contender for the mountains title alone. When he realized his mistake it was too late.

Unlike Poulidor, Zoetemelk would get his great moment, for in 1980 he went on to win the Tour de France. He had spent his professional career racing with Belgian and French teams without the success he wanted so badly, but then a British bicycle company set its sights on winning the Tour de France. They employed Peter Post, a shrewd Dutch manager, and all they needed in 1980 was a man capable of winning.

Raleigh Cycles had since 1974 been building a team that could one day win the Tour on a British-made bicycle, but although they had become the most feared formation in the sport, and had finished second in the Tour, they had not yet produced the winner. Post, a disciplinarian who had brought together a unit of riders whose loyalty to each other was unequalled, persuaded Zoetemelk to leave the Coop-Mercier team and join Raleigh. If he did so, Post promised, with the Raleigh team behind him, he would win the Tour. And Post never made empty promises!

The Raleigh team was made up of mostly Dutch and Belgian riders, and although most could — and did — win daily stages, there was no one capable of winning the Tour outright.

The addition of Zoetemelk now gave them a leader. Providing he could find the strength to lead in the mountains, they would make sure as a team that he lost no time in the important team time-trial, at which the flying Raleighs had no equal.

The 1980 Tour started in Frankfurt, with Bernard Hinault winning the prologue time-trial, but the Raleigh team took the race lead the next day when Gerrie Knetemann, their strong ex-world road champion with no thoughts on final victory, took the yellow jersey after the team won the team time-trial.

The race lead continued to change hands, and Hinault regained it from the Belgian Rudy Pevenage after the time-trial at La Plume in the south-west of France, where Zoetemelk had won the stage expected to have been Hinault's. The Frenchman only came fifth.

Although Hinault was leading overall, he was in real trouble. His efforts had increased the pain in his knee — he had a condition later diagnosed as tendonitis, for which the cure is rest and an operation, and he gave up the race after finishing at Pau the next day. Zoetemelk was left to start the next morning's stage to Luchon as the new leader with a time advantage over Pevenage of 1 minute 8 seconds. He refused to wear the yellow jersey left by Hinault until he had earned the right to it by winning it during the race. He had done this by the end of the day in Luchon; Joopy was in yellow.

Naturally, Zoetemelk had his detractors — people who said that if Hinault had not retired he would not have won — but he pointed out that the Tour was the toughest of all races, and Hinault's body had cried enough. His hadn't.

After Zoetemelk finally won his Tour he returned to his more familiar role as runner-up when he came second again in 1982, the race which found Hinault back in form, notching up his fifth win. Zoetemelk had had the day he had always dreamed of. However, after riding in sixteen Tours, the Dutchman can look back on the most envied record of them all: Ridden 16. Finished 16. In his last Tour, 1986, he finished a remarkable twenty-fourth but in 1987 — his forty-first year — he refused all the persuasions to do it just one more time.

Joop Zoetemelk was Holland's greatest rider, but not until he won the world title in 1985. Here, in the 1986 Tour he is wearing the rainbow jersey of world champion and belies his thirty-nine years and sixteen Tours de France!

'Younger riders should be given their chance to make it,' he said. 'I'm going to watch it at home on television.' In fact, he accepted an invitation from the organizers to Mont Ventoux to see the time-trial won by the new young French hope Jean-François Bernard.

On the barren, unusually cold Giant of Provence, Zoetemelk had come face to face with the new breed, but would they ever be able to look back in almost twenty years' time and be able to reflect on a career to equal that of Joop Zoetemelk?

Chapter 5
The English-speaking Arrivals

The Tour de France is no longer a typically French race and the days when the French riders won every year are gone — probably for ever — in what is certainly the most international of all of the world's stage races.

In 1988 the English language began to crackle through the Radio Tour air waves as results of mountain climbs were given in both English and German. (Until this year the Tour since its inception had only used French.) This was further proof that the Tour de France was accepting its own changing nature. In that year also the international trend continued unabated, and Canadian Steve Bauer won a stage, held the race lead and eventually finished a magnificent fourth overall.

These early pioneers had no support crews, just an urge to compete.

There were other English-speaking successes too, the most satisfying being that of likeable Sean Yates from Sussex, England, who won the time-trial from Liévin to Wasquehal in the fastest ever average speed recorded for such a stage. It was a great result for Yates and for Britain, continuing the process that began in 1937 when Charley Holland and Bill Burl became the first English riders to sign on for the Tour at *L'Auto*'s offices in Paris.

Until then there had been ten English-speaking riders, mostly Australian, who had attempted the race, and of these only Frankie Thomas had two goes, failing to finish both times.

The most noted effort was by Hubert 'Oppy' Opperman, who finished an excellent twelfth in 1931. Oppy was very popular, and not surprisingly his understanding of people and life in general was to help him become the Australian High Commissioner in Malta.

The early tours were indeed a challenge, but for very different reasons to those of the 1970s, when the publicity given to the race attracted demonstrations and terrorist outrages.

In 1937 the organizers allowed the use of *dérailleur* gears for the first time, so that instead of just one gear riders were able to choose from a multiple-geared system fitted to the rear wheels. There was another innovation too: each was also given a support car!

That year the ninety-eight riders entered as individuals or as members of national teams. These teams were very disparate in strength: Burl and Holland were grouped into a three-man team with the French-Canadian Pierre Gachon, while the big teams from France, Germany, Italy and Belgium had 10-man squads and all the fire-power needed to dominate the race. The two Englishmen hardly had a chance to meet Gachon because he lost his way on the opening stage between Paris and Lille (not difficult even today unless you use the motorway!) and failed to beat the time limit.

The race was also a baptism of fire for Burl, who was the first rider to crash. History is unclear as to whether he hit a spectator or another rider, but in any case it was a dreadful first stage for the trio. With the courage still evident among riders today, Burl continued on the second stage towards Charleville, when more problems, created by another crash, forced him outside the 15 per cent time limit (based on the winner's time) and out of the race. Only Holland was left — and the race had hardly begun.

Charley Holland, in contrast, was riding well among the top thirty, losing his high place only when accused of taking pace from a following support car on the Ballon d'Alsace. The new rule allowing following vehicles presented many fresh problems, and the cars often became entangled with the riders. Holland was said to have ridden behind one of them, and was relegated to the last place on the stage. He would not be among the twenty-six riders who returned to Paris. He was not beaten by the mountains either, but by a series of punctures that left him stranded.

Holland recalls: 'We were only allowed to carry two spare tyres, so I had to wait for something to turn up. A priest gave me a bottle of beer and it seemed ages before a tourist came along and gave me a tyre. The tyre kept coming off the rim so I found another, but by the time I arrived at Luchon the officials had gone. I took my number off and retired.' There were no further heroics from the British Isles, or indeed the Americas or Antipodes, for twenty-five years. Then the tide turned and the

Paul Sherwen, from Kelsall in Cheshire, called himself a 'super domestique' in the Tour de France. The likeable Englishman rode seven The likeable Englishman rode seven Tours, finishing five. Now he partners Phil Liggett on the Channel 4 commentary team.

steady progress towards the present English-speaking successes began.

In 1955, 130 riders assembled in Le Havre for the 4,855-km (3,010-mile) ride to nearby Paris, including the first full British team of ten riders, managed by Syd Cozens. This team had ridden regularly on the Continent, so were thought to be conditioned for the Tour. There were other innovations too, including the first use of photo-finish cameras, travelling bank facilities and the making of a film of every stage which was shown each evening to all the followers. Each of the 13 teams was given three cars — instead of the one of 1937 — and a van carrying spare parts.

Robert Millar is a quiet Scot whose legs do the talking. He was the first to win the Mountains title for Britain in 1984, and he'll be looking for it again in 1988. The possibility of winning the race outright as well is not just a dream in Millar's case!

That year the teams were composed from national and French regional squads, and the British colours were a white jersey with the Union Jack on each shoulder. The squad was sponsored by Hercules Bicycles. The team got off to a promising start, boosted by the fast stage-finishing of 'Ironman' Dave Bedwell, who now lives and works in Devon. Bedwell was barely five feet tall, but could produce tremendous turns of speed. As the race unfolded, though, the story became familiar, and the ten men dropped out until only Brian Robinson and Tony Hoar were left to finish in Paris.

Although the British team was unable to return in 1956 following the withdrawal of support from Hercules, the talented Robinson remained in France and found a place in a 'Luxembourg and foreigners' formation. This was led by Charly Gaul, whose victory was still to come. In the same team a young Irishman destined for stardom and tragedy — Shay Elliott — was also making his first appearance. This time Elliott retired, but Robinson finished a magnificent fourteenth after being third at one stage.

By the end of the 1950s, only the handful of English riders, and Shay Elliott, were still plugging away at the race, and in 1958 even Robinson failed to finish, though he created Tour history by becoming the first English rider to win a stage. He won the seventh between St Brieuc and Brest, the day after Elliott had taken second place going into St Brieuc. Actually, Robinson had not crossed the line first and had to appeal against the balking tactics of the Italian Arrigo Padovan in the sprint before being awarded the stage. But the Yorkshireman's great moment came when he closed the decade with one of the great individual rides of the Tour. Robinson, who had survived being eliminated early in the race when he was left back in on appeal, won the twentieth stage from Annecy to Châlon-sur-Saône by a massive margin of 20 min 6 sec!

The next decade started well with a full British team in 1960 which contained another future star in Tom Simpson, but Simpson and Robinson had little chance in their eight-man team, when the race had accepted others with as many as fourteen.

Simpson, only twenty-two, or 'Major Tom' to the French — was known for his carefree aggression. He was certainly no respecter of reputations, and was soon among the pace-setters. After just three days he was in a position to take the yellow jersey.

He was on course to be in yellow when the race arrived at Ostend, but he had underestimated the French riders who had the majority in the leading group. Simpson needed to finish second and win a 30-second bonus to take the lead, but instead he was third and the dream was back on file! He said of the 1960 Tour: 'Those last ten days were agony and ridden almost on will-power alone. Robinson tried to help with words of encouragement, but I was past help and just could not be bothered to listen. When I finished the Tour de France, I never wanted to ride another one.'

In 1961 there were nine Englishmen, two Irishmen and a Scot in what was the biggest attempt to ride well in the race. Men like Simpson and Robinson had already proved themselves, and rugged talent like Kenny Laidlaw from Glasgow was welcomed.

The three finishers represented England, Scotland and Ireland, but although Great Britain was able to say that a team had finished for the first time, it could strictly speaking claim only Robinson and Laidlaw, since Elliott was a Dubliner.

Running concurrently in 1961 was the new Tour de l'Avenir, which was a race for amateurs, and which had shorter stages over fewer days. Riding well in it was an Englishman, Alan Ramsbottom, whose rimless spectacles made him look a most unlikely athlete. However, in 1962 it would be Simpson and Ramsbottom who would be the stars of the Tour de France.

It is significant that all the home riders who succeeded in the Tour had made their homes in France or Belgium. There was no popping back home when the going got tough.

All the dedication and determination to succeed finally paid off and in 1962 — twenty-five years after Charley Holland and Bill Burl had led the way for British riders — Tom Simpson became the first Briton to pull on the Maillot Jaune.

The organizers were experimenting constantly (things have not changed today), and that year they had reverted back to trade teams. Among the British only Simpson (Gitane Bicycles) and Ramsbottom (Pelforth Beers) had ridden well enough to gain selection for their teams. Both finished, while Simpson scored the best final overall position to date, arriving in sixth place. Ramsbottom was forty-fifth.

Simpson's (and Britain's) greatest moment in the Tour had come on the fourteenth stage from Pau to St Gaudens in the Pyrenees. The brilliant Tom finished with a strong group of riders after they had scaled the Col du Tourmalet, Aspin and Peyresourde (a similar stage to the one planned for this year) and had enough time in hand to pull on the yellow jersey.

The very next day was a time-trial from Luchon up to the top of Superbagnères, and he had no chance to recuperate, his lead passing after the 18.5-km test to Jef Planckaert from Belgium. His final sixth place had left him confident that he had the ability to win the race one day, although fate was to ensure that he would not.

In 1963 Shay Elliott matched Simpson by taking the yellow jersey for Ireland and keeping it for four days, while Ramsbottom continued to develop by finishing sixteenth overall. Simpson, after winning the Bordeaux—Paris one-day classic, had decided not to ride.

A few hours' notice, and New Zealander Nathan Dahlberg found himself in the 1988 Tour for the first time. He wasn't expected to finish, but he rode with all the courage of a seasoned rider, to win the admiration of all.

Robinson had now retired, but strong riders were still emerging: Ramsbottom, Simpson, Barry Hoban, Vin Denson and Michael Wright were all enjoying France's greatest race. Wright was a novelty, not just to the French but to the English themselves. He spoke only French, for his family had moved from Bishop's Stortford in Hertfordshire to Belgium when he was only six years old. He had retained his British passport, which qualified him for the team that formed for the 1967 race when selection was again on a national basis.

Simpson chose a team of riders mainly experienced in Europe, as he felt 1967 was the year for a serious attempt at winning the Tour. He was now twenty-nine.

The team started full of hope and in buoyant mood, but instead of the year ending in British victory, Tom Simpson died on Mont Ventoux on the thirteenth stage on 13 July. The late Jock Wadley had vivid memories of that day in the Provence inferno, when temperatures soared, and he wrote afterwards:

I watched the whole field go by on Mont Ventoux, but no Tom, then I was told the poor lad had collapsed. In the Press room dozens of journalists from all nationalities were in

In 1962 Tom Simpson became the first Briton to pull on the maillot jaune.

Opposite: *Tom Simpson did what everyone thought impossible. In 1962 he became the only British rider to wear the yellow jersey at St Gaudens in the Pyrenees, losing it the very next day near Luchon.*

tears. Terrible enough that any rider should have lost his life, but it was a matter of personal distress that the Ventoux had taken not just a champion, but a friend of us all.

The loss of Britain's only professional world road-racing champion had also meant the loss for the foreseeable future of a home winner, and even today people talk about the need 'for a Simpson' in the British sport.

Barry Hoban — who was allowed by the rest of the race to win the next stage in Simpson's memory — Arthur Metcalfe and Colin Lewis went on to finish the race in Paris. Another rider, Vin Denson, could not recover morale after the loss of his great friend and retired.

With the approach of the 1970s Britain relied heavily on Barry Hoban for success, and he did not disappoint. He won in all eight stages, and eventually married Tom Simpson's widow Helen. Both live happily now in Wales and retain an interest in the sport. Barry still leads the home stage winners' table by a good margin.

1978 was the year of Hoban's last Tour. Despite the arrival of a chirpy Paul Sherwen (who retired in 1987 to manage the Raleigh—Banana Group team after seven Tours), the English-speaking world was now focusing on Ireland.

Shay Elliot had retired and then, following emotional and personal distress, committed suicide. The sport had lost a most likeable man who would have revelled in the successes of the new star from Ireland, Sean Kelly. Kelly entered the professional world almost by default after being banned from competing in the 1976 Olympic Games because he had raced in South Africa.

With no Olympics to work for he moved to France and Italy, and immediately started winning big amateur races. The team he finally joined was Flandria, managed by a French Viscount, Jean de Gribaldy. This man — he died in 1987 — would watch over Kelly throughout his professional career.

Today, Kelly is still trying to win the Tour de France. The farm labourer from Carrick-on-Suir appeared at first to be just a sprinter, and he proved this by winning his first stage in 1978, but since then he has improved so much, especially in the time-trial, that for some years now he has been seen as a potential Tour winner.

Kelly's ten attempts to win the Tour de France have given him both his happiest and his saddest moments. His stage victories in 1978 and 1980 made him Ireland's top sportsman, and the yellow jersey which he wore for a day after finishing third in Pau in 1983 recalled Shay Elliott. He has won Paris—Nice an incredible seven consecutive times, taking the record away from Jacques Anquetil. He has won the Tour of Switzerland, and last season added the Tour of Spain to his victories — but will he ever win the Tour de France?

Until 1988 Davis Phinney had won stages but never completed the Tour. This time — his third attempt — he arrived in Paris by bike instead of by car!

Kelly has won the green points jersey three times; once more and he would hold another record, but he is not interested. At thirty-three, time is running out, but he would be a very popular winner in 1989.

In 1984 — a historic year for the English-speakers, with four in the top ten — Kelly came fifth. He improved a year later to fourth, but the Irish newcomer Stephen Roche was third.

From now on Roche, a loquacious Dubliner, was to be the headline-maker, and Kelly was to continue as the world's most consistent rider, but without a good Tour performance as proof.

The 1980s have seen a great infusion of riders from America, Australia and Canada, and in 1981 Jonathan Boyer became the first American to finish the race. Before retiring in 1987, achieved a great result when he came twelfth in 1983.

The Tour no longer accepts national teams, so since 1969 there has been no opportunity to enter a full national squad, but there have been plenty of outstanding individual performances by the English-speakers, usually in foreign teams. The only exception to this was the entry by the ANC–Halfords team in 1987, which proved to be an ego trip for the company who had secured the sponsorship and a battle for survival by those who rode.

The nearest Britain has come to finding a new Tom Simpson is Robert Millar, a Scot married to a French girl, who has the most enviable talent of being able to climb mountains. Millar is a difficult person to get to know, but his quiet, introverted manner changes when he sits on the saddle! In 1984 Millar produced the ride of his life by not only finishing fourth overall — a British best — but by becoming the first English-speaker to win the King of the Mountains title.

In 1988 Millar hated being referred to as the leader of his Spanish (French-based) Fagor team during the Tour, and after losing the stage at Guzet Neige because of a confused finish, his morale ebbed until he retired.

He has twice finished second in the Tour of Spain and once in the Tour of Italy. At thirty he can still win the Tour de France, and remains Britain's only realistic hope.

But let us go back to 1981 when 'British' hopes rested with Australian Phil Anderson, who had left these shores when only a year old.

Anderson, a former Commonwealth Games champion, finished tenth in his first Tour in 1981 (two places better than Opperman in 1931). After wearing the yellow jersey in the Pyrenees for a day, he moved quickly into the highly paid ranks of professional riders.

Anderson was back in 1982, this time finishing fifth in what was a marvellous Tour for him. He wore the yellow jersey for nine days, and then ended up with the white jersey as the best-placed young rider.

He was also fifth in 1985, but now that he is thirty-one he will have a tough fight to come back. Anderson's team was not selected for the Tour last year, which was sad, as he enjoyed a great year with places in the single-day classic races and a win in the Tour of Denmark.

The performances of all the English-speaking riders listed at the end of this chapter show the increased interest in the Tour. This is especially so in the case of the Americans, who have taken the race seriously in the last five years, and have enjoyed enormous success.

Californian Greg LeMond made an impressive start to his Tour career in 1984, when he finished third. The next year he was second, and in 1986 he won! His second place in 1985 is recalled in Chapter 3, during his battle with Bernard Hinault, and when the 1986 edition came around LeMond intended to make sure he would win the race.

In 1986 the two riders were again both on the same team and both seemed bitter rivals, which made for a great race. Hinault gave nothing, often causing LeMond to question openly whose side he was on. LeMond admitted he used to lie awake at night trying to work out his rival's thoughts. Did he want to win the race himself or was he going to help LeMond win it?

Things happened then that hadn't happened for years in a Tour de France — take the twelfth stage from Bayonne to Pau, a long ride of 217 km, for example. By the end of the stage Hinault had given his all to gain a massive 4 minutes 36 seconds over LeMond, who trailed in in third place.

'It's all over,' said LeMond, but was it? The very next day the race finished like this at the ski station of Superbagnères: 1. LeMond. 2. Millar at 1 m in 12 sec. 11. Hinault at 4 min 39 sec.

This was no ordinary Tour. Hinault was still the leader, but LeMond was now only 40 seconds behind.

The animosity between the two former friends remained. LeMond finished third in the Alps at the top of the viciously steep Col du Granon, at the end of the 190-km stage from Gap. He was almost three minutes ahead of Hinault, winning the yellow jersey at last.

With the Tour now seemingly set for its first American winner, the cruel climb up the twists of Alpe d'Huez provided another unusual and memorable sight. LeMond and Hinault not only fled the field together but finished over five minutes in front as a partnership, with LeMond holding Hinault's arm aloft as they crossed the line.

Hinault then declared that if he did not defeat LeMond in the time-trial at St Etienne he would concede the race and see that the American won. Although he won the time-trial, he gained only 25 seconds, but even this victory came amid hysterical accusations of sabotage when LeMond's brakes came loose and he crashed and changed machines. No one who knew

Hinault would ever have accused him of such underhanded tactics, and LeMond himself wasn't doing so either, but the pressure of the American and his close followers — always under the eye of CBS television cameras — was almost unendurable.

At the finish in Paris, amid the emotion of the first Tour victory for an English-speaker — and an American at that — both men declared themselves to be again the best of friends. Hinault made sure of having a winner's jersey on the podium too, for as soon as he had conceded the Tour he went for the King of the Mountains jersey instead!

In 1987 Stephen Roche continued where Greg LeMond left off, while the American quickly fell away from the headlines after a broken wrist was followed by a shooting accident while hunting which left him unable to defend his title. Last year LeMond returned to the front line with his new PDM team, but after a mediocre season the American has not yet proved that he can ever return to be the rider of 1986. The same has to be said of Stephen Roche. Following a season dogged with injury and dissension with his Fagor team, 1988 has been thoroughly forgettable for Roche. However, a glance at his career since 1981 shows him to have incredibly successful seasons in alternate years — so roll on 1989!

But first we should remember Roche as the first Irish winner of the Tour de France in 1987, which when added to his victories the same season in the Tour of Italy and world championship equalled the exploits of Eddy Merckx in 1974, the only

The line of washing all riders would love, but only two have got! Stephen Roche matched the 1974 record of Eddy Merckx when, in 1987, he won the Tour de France (yellow jersey) world championship (white) and the Tour of Italy.

other rider to accomplish cycling's Grand Slam. Roche, after coming in third in his first Tour in 1985, finished an undistinguished forty-eighth in 1986, and in the winter underwent surgery to cure a knee problem that had been threatening his career. His win in the Tour of Italy in June of 1987 indicated he was back to his old self. He arrived in Berlin for the Tour de France start knowing that the double was possible — something only four riders had done. Fausto Coppi, Jacques Anquetil, Merckx and Hinault were only members of an élite club.

Roche started well by finishing third in the Prologue and then confirmed his form by winning the longest time-trial for thirty-six years — 87 km between Saumur and Poitiers. He was sixth, over three minutes behind France's Charly Mottet, but with all the mountains still to come. On Mont Ventoux he faced a set-back when Jean-François Bernard won the time-trial, but even so, he had improved to second overall, 2 – 34 behind the Frenchman. Immediately after the stage finish Roche predicted that the race was not finished, and he was right.

Next day Bernard's chain jammed and he lost the yellow jersey as Roche, and Spain's Pedro Delgado, raced clear to finish at Villard de Lans well ahead. Delgado won, and Roche became only the third Irishman to lead the race. But Roche predicted more changes, and again he was right. Delgado was a magnificent competitor, and on Alpe d'Huez — where he had given up, distressed by the sudden death of his mother, the previous year — the Spaniard was to have his finest hour in the Tour. He finished seventh, taking the yellow jersey from Roche by just 25 seconds. It was a poignant moment in the Tour and not just a sad day for Ireland as Delgado remembered his mother.

Sean Yates became the fastest ever time-triallist in the Tour de France, and Britain's first ever winner on such a stage when he won at Wasquehal last year.

All those watching the 1987 Tour on television in Britain and Ireland will remember the next day's stage to La Plagne, farther along the Alpine roads from Bourg d'Oisans. Delgado knew his time was running out. If he was to win the race he needed a 'buffer' of two minutes before the final time-trial at Dijon, so he attacked and gambled everything. At first he left his rival Roche and gained more than his two minutes, but then he slowed dramatically and Roche recovered from a seemingly hopeless situation.

The Tour de France is littered throughout its history with tales of superhuman effort, but the effort made by Roche on this twenty-first day was to be one of the most memorable. 'You can say I didn't win the Tour today, but I haven't lost it either,' said the Irishman some time after he had been given lengthy gulps of oxygen after collapsing at the mountain-top finish.

Delgado had played his cards and almost won, but he was to wait another year before winning the race. This time he had made a great effort to finish just four seconds ahead of Roche at La Plagne, saying then, 'When I crossed the line and looked back to see Roche, I knew I'd lost the Tour.' The Dijon time-trial was a formality, and Roche beat him by 61 seconds, to win the race by just 40, the second closest finish of them all.

In 1987 Ireland enjoyed its most memorable sporting year and Roche was made a Freeman of his home city of Dublin — the first sportsman to receive the honour — but in 1988 it was all change again for Stephen Roche.

The knee injury that was thought to have been cleared up came back, and the new world champion, Tour de France and Tour of Italy winner was sidelined for practically all the season. No defence in Italy, and certainly no defence in France, left Roche with low morale, but with one hope for 1989. Ironically, just before the Tour de France started Roche's knee problem was finally cleared up, too late to prepare a defence of his title, but with great hopes for the following year.

Instead, Pedro Delgado finally won the race he has so richly deserved. The suspicion of doping has certainly marred his win, although in Spain it was seen as a French trick to deprive the first Spanish winner since Luis Ocana in 1973 of his finest hour. It was also another great Tour for the English-speakers, and Steve Bauer from Canada — who has threatened to win a major race since he took the silver medal in Los Angeles Olympic Games in 1984 — finally matured.

Bauer, from Fenwick, Ontario, was not being seen as a long-term challenger in 1988, even after he won the opening road-race stage at Machecoul. But once in the yellow jersey at Nancy after eight days, he became a new man, receiving all the inspiration that the yellow jersey seems to give a leader.

Bauer took the lead off Dutchman Jelle Nijdam by just 10 seconds, and he never lost it until the second day in the Alps when Delgado took the *maillot jaune* on Alpe d'Huez. Bauer never really expected to win, and continued to fight for a top finish. Despite the climbs, he defied some of the best climbers to eventually finish fourth — the highest ever by a Canadian.

Great Britain also continued its own successes with Sean Yates time-trialling to his memorable win at Wasquehal, and Robert Millar adding another of his famous Pyrenean raids to his record. Millar will not remember this one with fondness, though, as he failed to turn left at the top of Guzet Neige, thinking the gendarme's signal was for the following cars, and lost the stage win. Instead he finished second, and retired later on the road to Limoges.

Sheffield's Malcolm Elliott continued his best season in Europe by narrowly missing a stage success and finishing his second Tour in ninetieth place, but the most remarkable performance came from New Zealand's Nathan Dahlberg. Dahlberg received just 12 hours' notice to start the Tour when the 7-Eleven team lost Bob Roll in an accident when warming up for the pre-race team time-trial.

The team felt that since they had lost one of their strong 'work-horses' it would be better to start with a full squad, even if the rider did not make it to the finish in Paris, so an SOS went to Dahlberg's Belgian lodgings. The New Zealander didn't believe it at first when he was told to pack his bag and be in Brittany by the morning he was riding the Tour de France!

Showing the resilience of a much-travelled man (he was only twenty-three, by the way!) Dahlberg travelled through the night and was soon in the thick of the race, learning as he went, but saying openly that he would not be around when the mountains came as his reserves were being used up on the flat stages!

Nathan Dahlberg finished 144th, earning the respect of everyone who came to know him.

Below is a list of all the English-speaking riders who have attempted the race. The figures in parenthesis indicate any stages they won. Zeros against a rider's name indicate a non-finisher; other preceeding figurs show overall placings.

1914
17 Don Kirkham — Aust
20 Munro — Aust

1928
28 Harry Watson — NZ
38 Percy Osbourne — Aust
0 Ernest Bainbridge — Aust
0 Frankie Thomas — Aust

1929
0 Adolphe Cockx — USA

1931
12 Humbert Opperman — Aust
35 Richard Lamb — Aust
0 Ossie Nicholson — Aust
0 Frankie Thomas — Aust

1937
0 Bill Burl — Engl
0 Charles Holland — Eng

1952
0 John Beasley — Aust

1955
29 Brian Robinson — Eng
64 Russell Mockridge — Aust
69 Tony Hoar — Eng
0 John Beasley — Aust
0 Dave Bedwell — Eng
0 Stan Jones — Eng
0 Fred Krebs — Eng
0 Bob Maitland — Eng
0 Ken Mitchell — Eng
0 Bernard Pusey — Eng
0 Ian Steel — Eng
0 Bev Wood — Eng

1956
14 Brian Robinson — Eng
86 Reg Arnold — Aust
0 Shay Elliott — Ire

1957
0 Brian Robinson — Eng

1958
48 Shay Elliott — Ire
69 Stan Brittain — Eng
0 Ron Coe — Eng
0 Brian Robinson — Eng (7)

1959
19 Brian Robinson — Eng (20)
37 Vic Sutton — Eng
0 John Andrews — Eng
0 Shay Elliott — Ire
0 Tony Hewson — Eng

1960
26 Brian Robinson — Eng
29 Tom Simpson — Eng
0 John Andrews — Eng
0 Stan Brittain — Eng
0 John Kennedy — Eng
0 Harry Reynolds — Eng
0 Normal Sheil — Eng
0 Vic Sutton — Eng

1961
47 Shay Elliott — Ire
53 Brian Robinson — Eng
65 Ken Laidlaw — Scot
 0 Stan Brittain — Eng
 0 Ron Coe — Eng
 0 Vin Denson — Eng
 0 Albert Hitchen — Eng
 0 Ian Moore — Ire
 0 George O'Brien — Eng
 0 Pete Ryall — Eng
 0 Sean Ryan — Eng
 0 Tom Simpson — Eng

1962
 6 Tom Simpson — Eng
45 Alan Ramsbottom —
 Eng

1963
16 Alan Ramsbottom —
 Eng
61 Shay Elliott — Ire (3)

1964
14 Tom Simpson — Eng
56 Michael Wright — Eng
65 Barry Hoban — Eng
72 Vin Denson — Eng
 0 Shay Elliott — Ire

1965
24 Michael Wright — Eng
 (2)
87 Vin Denson — Eng
 0 Tom Simpson — Eng

1966
 0 Vin Denson — Eng
 0 Tom Simpson — Eng

1967
62 Barry Hoban — Eng
 (14)
69 Arthur Metcalfe — Eng
84 Colin Lewis — Eng
 0 Pete Chisman — Eng
 0 Vin Denson — Eng
 0 Peter Hill — Eng
 0 Albert Hitchen — Eng
 0 Bill Lawrie — Aust
 0 Tom Simpson — Eng
 0 Michael Wright — Eng
 (7)

1968
28 Michael Wright — Eng
33 Barry Hoban — Eng
 (19)
62 Vin Denson — Eng
63 John Clarey — Eng
 0 Bob Addy — Eng
 0 Derek Green — Eng
 0 Derek Harrison — Eng
 0 Colin Lewis — Eng
 0 Arthur Metcalfe — Eng
 0 Hugh Porter — Eng

1969
32 Derek Harrison — Eng
67 Barry Hoban — Eng (18
 & 19)
71 Michael Wright — Eng

1970
 0 Barry Hoban — Eng

1971
40 Barry Hoban — Eng

1972
55 Michael Wright — Eng
 (10)
70 Barry Hoban — Eng

1973
43 Barry Hoban — Eng (11
 & 19)
57 Michael Wright — Eng

1974
 37 Barry Hoban — Eng
 (13)
 57 Michael Wright — Eng
103 Don Allan — Aust

1975
68 Barry Hoban — Eng (8)
85 Don Allan — Aust

1977
 0 Bill Nickson — Eng

1978
34 Sean Kelly — Ire (6)
65 Barry Hoban — Eng
70 Paul Sherwen — Eng

1979
38 Sean Kelly — Ire
82 Paul Sherwen — Eng
 0 Paul Jesson — NZ

1980
29 Sean Kelly — Ire (19 &
 21)
49 Graham Jones — Eng
 0 Paul Sherwen — Eng

1981
10 Phil Anderson — Aust
20 Graham Jones — Eng
32 Jonathan Boyer — USA
48 Sean Kelly — Ire (15)
 0 Paul Sherwen — Eng

1982
 5 Phil Anderson — Aust
 (2)
 15 Sean Kelly — Ire (12)
 23 Jonathan Boyer —
 USA
 87 Eric McKenzie — NZ
111 Paul Sherwen — Eng

1983
 7 Sean Kely — Ire
 9 Phil Anderson — Aust
12 Jonathan Boyer — USA
13 Stephen Roche — Ire
14 Robert Millar — Scot
 (10)
69 Graham Jones — Eng
 0 Eric McKenzie — NZ

1984
 3 Greg LeMond — USA
 4 Robert Millar — Scot
 (11)
 5 Sean Kelly — Ire
 10 Phil Anderson — Aust
 25 Stephen Roche — Ire
 31 Jonathan Boyer —
 USA
 91 Sean Yates — Eng
 95 Allan Peiper — Aust
116 Paul Sherwen — Eng
 0 Graham Jones — Eng

1985

2 Greg LeMond — USA (21

3 Stephen Roche — Ire (18a)

4 Sean Kelly — Ire

5 Phil Anderson — Aust

10 Steve Bauer — Can

11 Robert Millar — Scot

74 Doug Shapiro — USA

86 Allan Peiper — Aust

122 Sean Yates — Eng

127 Eric McKenzie — NZ

141 Paul Sherwen — Eng

1986

1 Greg LeMond — USA (13)

4 Andy Hampsten — USA

23 Steve Bauer — Can

39 Phil Anderson — Aust

48 Stephen Roche — Ire

63 Bob Roll — USA

80 Jeff Pierce — USA

96 Ron Kiefel — USA

112 Sean Yates — Eng

120 Alex Stieda — Can

131 Paul Kimmage — Ire

0 Chris Carmichael — USA

0 Alexi Grewal — USA

0 Eric Heiden — USA

0 Eric McKenzie — NZ

0 Robert Millar — Scot

0 Davis Phinney — USA (3)

0 Doug Shapiro — USA

1987

1 Stephen Roche — Ire (1)

16 Andy Hampsten — USA

19 Robert Millar — Scot

27 Phil Anderson — Aust

65 Martin Earley — Ire

70 Adrian Timmis — Eng

74 Steve Bauer — Can

82 Ron Kiefel — USA

88 Jeff Pierce — USA (25)

94 Malcolm Elliott — Eng

98 Jonathan Boyer — USA

0 Jeff Bradley — USA

0 Graham Jones — Eng

0 Sean Kelly — Ire

0 Paul Kimmage — Ire

0 Davis Phinney — USA (12)

0 Allan Peiper — Aust

0 Bob Roll — USA

0 Shane Sutton — Aust

0 Paul Watson — Eng

0 Sean Yates — Eng

1988

4 Steve Bauer — Can (1)

15 Andy Hampsten — USA

46 Sean Kelly — Ire

50 Michael Wilson — Aust

59 Sean Yates — Eng (6)

90 Malcolm Elliott — Eng

135 Andy Bishop — USA

144 Nathan Dahlberg — N.Z.

0 Martin Earley — Ire

0 Roy Knickman — USA

0 Robert Millar — Scot

0 Jeff Pierce — USA

Winners of Yellow Jersey

Tom Simpson, the only Englishman to lead the race in 1962.

Phil Anderson, the only Australian in 1981.

Greg LeMond, the only American to win in 1986.

Alex Stieda, the first Canadian to lead the race in 1986. Steve Bauer joined him in 1988.

Shay Elliott was the first Irishman to lead the race in 1963, followed by Sean Kelly in 1983 and Stephen Roche, the first Irish winner, in 1987.

Those who Race to Win in 1989

Steve Bauer — Canada
Born: 12 June 1959
From: Fenwick, Ontario, lives Belgium.
Years professional: 5
World ranking at start of season: 6
Tour performances:
  1985 — 10th
  1986 — 23rd
  1987 — 74th
  1988 — 4th

Other major performances:
1984 — 2nd Olympic road race Los Angeles.
3rd World professional road race Championship, Spain.
1985 — 9th World championship, Italy.
1986 — 4th Tour of Flanders.
2nd Tour of Ireland (Nissan Classic).
1987 — 4th Tour of Flanders.
10th Tour of Italy.
13th World championship, Austria.
1988 — 2nd Tour of Switzerland.
1st Stage 1, Tour de France and leader.

Comment: Steve Bauer is a quiet, serious rider who has the determination and drive to succeed. His season last year was marred near the end, when he was disqualified from second place in the world road race championship in Ronse, Belgium, after he allegedly caused Claude Criquielion to fall, 75 metres from the line.

Steve Bauer became only the second Canadian to take the race lead in 1988 and the first to win a stage. He went on to finish a magnificent fourth in Paris.

Sean Kelly — Ireland
Born: 24 May 1956
From: Carrick-on-Suir;
lives in Belgium.
Years professional: 11
*World ranking at start of
season:* 1
Tour performances:
1978 — 34th
1979 — 38th
1980 — 29th
1981 — 48th
1982 — 15th
1983 — 7th
1984 — 5th
1985 — 4th
1987 — Crashed and
retired.
1988 — 46th

*Other major
performances:*
1977 — 2nd Tour of
Holland.
16th World Championship,
Venezuela.
1978 — First Tour de
France stage win at
Poitiers.
1979 — 9th World
championship, Holland.
1980 — Five stage wins
and Points jersey, Tour of
Spain.
1981 — 4th Flèche
Wallonne.
42nd World championship,
Czechoslovakia.
1982 — Paris—Nice — the
first of seven consecutive
wins. Green Points jersey,
Tour de France — first of
three wins.
3rd World championship,
Goodwood, England.
1983 — Tour of
Switzerland.
Yellow Jersey in Tour de
France for only time to
date.
8th World championship,
Switzerland.
Tour of Lombardy (First
classic win).

1984 — Paris—Roubaix.
Liège—Bastogne—Liège.
1985 -- Tour of Ireland
(Nissan Classic) — first of
three wins.
Tour of Lombardy.
Pernod Trophy (France's
top international award).
35th World championship,
Italy.
1986 — Milan—San Remo.
Paris—Roubaix.
3rd Tour of Spain and
points Jersey.
5th World championship.
GP des Nations.
1987 — Tour of the Basque
Country.
2nd Tour of Flanders.
5th World championship.
1988 — Paris—Nice for
seventh time.
Ghent—Wevelgem.
Tour of Spain.
3rd Kellogg's Tour of
Britain.
25th World championship,
Belgium.

Comment: Kelly has
achieved most things in
the sport except the world
title or the Tour de
France; he has come close
in both. Time is running
out for him to win the
Tour, but he will keep
trying and hoping. He has
two great assets; he is
rarely ill, and he has a
marvellous mental
approach — the harder
the going the more Kelly
enjoys it. He has not won
a stage since 1982, and
that will be a sure target
this year.

Stephen Roche — Ireland.
Born: 28 November 1959.
From: Dublin, lives France.
Years professional: 7
*World ranking at start of
season:* 43
Tour performances:
1983 — 13th
1984 — 25th
1985 — 3rd
1986 — 48th
1987 — 1st

*Other major
performances:*
1981 — Paris—Nice (First
Irish winner).
1982 — 2nd Amstel Gold
Race.
1983 — Tour of Romandy.
3rd world championship,
Switzerland.
1984 — 2nd Paris—Nice.
Tour of Romandy.
1985 — First stage win in
the Tour de France.
7th world championship,
Italy.
1987 — Tour of Romandy.
Tour of Italy.
World championship,
Austria.
1988 — 6th Kellogg's Tour
of Britain.
76th World championship,
Belgium.

Comment: Last year was
very disappointing for
Stephen, after he broke all
records in 1987. His knee
injury at last seems cured,
and he finished the season
racing, but looking
forward to the new season
to follow. There was
proof of a full recovery
when he won the Tour of
the Basque Country in
Spain this April, but like
Greg LeMond, Roche
knows that the road back
is long and hard.

Andy Hampsten — United States of America
Born: 7 April 1962.
From: Boulder, Colorado.
Years professional: 5
World ranking at start of season: 16
Tour Performances:
    1986 — 4th
    1987 — 16th
    1988 — 15th

Other major performances:
1985 — 20th Tour of Italy and stage win.
64th World championship, Italy.
1986 — Tour of Switzerland.
Best young rider in Tour de France (White jersey).
1987 — Tour of Switzerland.
45th World championship, Austria.
1988 — Tour of Italy.

Comment: In four seasons, ever-smiling Andy Hampsten has become America's No. 2 rider, beaten only by Greg LeMond. He will be a real favourite to win the Tour this year, but then he might be unable to defend his Tour of Italy title, as few riders can perform well in both races.

Robert Millar — Scotland
Born: 13 September 1958.
From: Glasgow, lives France.
Years professional: 8
World ranking at start of season: 23
Tour performances:
    1983 — 14th
    1984 — 4th
    1985 — 11th
    1987 — 19th

Other major performances:
1980 — 11th World championship, France.
1981 — 14th World championship, Czechoslovakia.
1982 — 2nd Tour de l'Avenir.
1983 — Stage win Tour de France in Luchon.
1984 — Leader Paris—Nice and 6th in the end.
Stage win Tour de France at Guzet—Neige.
Stage win in Midi Libre and 4th in the end.
King of the Mountains Tour de France (First for GB).
6th World championship, Spain.
1985 — 2nd Tour of Spain.
3rd King of the Mountains, Tour de France.
Tour of Catalonia.
10th World championship, Italy.
1986 — 2nd Tour of Spain, and leader for four days.
2nd Tour of Switzerland.
1987 — 2nd Tour of Italy and King of the Mountains.
1988 — 3rd Liège—Bastogne—Liège.
6th Tour of Spain.
49th World championship, Belgium.

Comment: Robert's record is the finest ever by a British rider, and can be compared only with Tom Simpson's, who excelled in other races, such as the single-day classics and world championship. He is a quiet rider, often taciturn, but always tries to give of his best — largely to prove to himself that he can do it. After last year's Tour he seemed to believe that he was no longer a candidate for victory, but another year is here, and Robert will again be a challenger. His record shows he has the ability.

Chapter 6
The Demands

Riders in the Tour de France no longer take part singly for the glory of winning — they also take part for the high monetary stakes. Very soon (perhaps next year), the Tour will boast a million pounds in prize money. There is no doubt that the race, even when taken out of context, is exhausting, and few riders ever return to win again. Greg LeMond and Stephen Roche might be proving that fact right now. But when you consider the Tour de France in the context of the rest of the world calendar, you realize just how exhausting the race really is. The organizers claim to have recognized this in 1989 and reduced the race distance despite increasing the days. The last week is described by them as 'feeble mileage', but the terrain is anything but!

A professional rider's season starts in February and ends in October — if he has not been sick or injured — and during that time he may have pedalled in 150 races and totalled over 18,000 miles! It is fair to say that although all would like to race for the money, many still do so for love of the sport. Just to ride in the Tour de France is the pinnacle of any rider's ambition, to finish it is worthy of the highest praise and to win is beyond the wildest dreams of most riders.

The youngest rider ever to start the Tour was the seventeen-year-old Frenchman Filly (Christian name unknown), who took part in the 1904 Tour. Although he did not then complete the course, the next year he finished in fourteenth place!

The oldest rider was the fifty-year-old Paret, another Frenchman, who finished in eleventh place in 1904. But these are the extremes. Nowadays no coach would allow a rider to contemplate the race before the age of twenty-three — preferably twenty-four. How long you go on is a question of mental attitude as well as physical condition. The amazing enthusiasm of Poulidor and Zoetemelk kept them on the finish podium until they were forty. Even Britain's Barry Hoban was at one stage the doyen of the bunch, riding his last Tour at the age of thirty-eight.

Modern racing is far more challenging than it has ever been. You can see the demands made on professional riders by looking at the selection from the 1989 programme of major events given at the end of this chapter.

The team leaders will want to perform well in the top races — the Tours of Italy, France, Spain — as well as in a selection of single-day classic races and the world road-race championship. These are the races that command the most exposure in the Press, on radio and television, where the sponsor expects his return for an annual expenditure on a team that could be in excess of a million pounds. The team *domestiques* (the riders who will be expected to sacrifice all to help the leaders win the big races) also have ambitions of their own, and if they feel they have the ability they will not be satisfied to remain team helpers, where financial reward is far less than that received by a star. Besides helping their team leaders get the results to keep the sponsors happy, they will also try to win themselves.

All this places a great deal of strain on a young rider who is aiming high. In order to become a professional in the first place a rider will have been successful as an amateur at either international level (which means he has represented his country) or by winning top races in either France, Belgium, Italy or Holland, the countries most prominent in the sport, and where note is taken of the really talented youngsters. Eddy Merckx and Greg LeMond were both world champions before they turned professional, but there have also been those who found their own sponsers *before* proving themselves good enough for the big teams later. These are the exceptions.

The professional *peloton* (the French word for race field), does not tolerate newcomers lightly, especially in the Tour de France. All riders must first serve their apprenticeship, and unless you are possessed with the extraordinary ability of an Eddy Merckx, will be expected to learn the rules. The veterans of the pack — riders who have ridden professionally for many seasons — have learned when to force the pace and when to save their energy. These riders, often team leaders, advise their young charges how to conserve their strengths, teaching them where to place themselves in the field to avoid the wind or generally save energy. Young riders being built up for the hard years to come are sometimes advised to compete in some single-day races up until the halfway point, and then 'abandon' — even if they feel good enough to finish! This way they are building up their stamina rather than exhausting their bodies.

Jacques Anquetil set quite a trend in 1965 when, two hours after winning the Dauphiné–Libéré stage race, he chartered an aeroplane with his French team to fly to Bordeaux. Only nine hours after finishing the Dauphiné–Libéré event, he was taking part in the longest single-day classic from Bordeaux to Paris, a ride of 557 km. He went on to win the race in a unique double victory that still stands.

Nowadays such schedules are almost routine for the top riders. A phone-call from a rider's manager and he will be at the airport, bike in hand, with just the name of his hotel in his pocket. He may ride a three hours' race and be on the next flight home — it is just a day's work!

It is easy to understand how such an arduous season could be a recipe for disaster for a young and inexperienced rider, leaving him exhausted by June. Because of this long timespan, and the demands on teams and riders to travel to many different countries, the world body is continually monitoring the international calendar. For example, all stage races are restricted to a maximum of 260 km a day and an average of 180 km for the race period.

Shelly Verses was the first masseuse to work on the Tour de France. Here Shelly breaks down the lactic acid in Janus Kuum's legs.

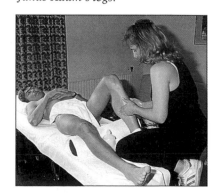

The mountains are dangerous, and the descents feared by the riders. This accident to Henrick Davos ended his Tour and he had a helicopter ride to hospital.

Doping

Sadly, the Olympic Games in Seoul — for those who were not there — will be remembered as the Games of the doped athletes. For the first time, ordinary people in their millions were forced to accept that in a major sporting contest, because of the rewards, cheating was prevalent. More importantly, the people who have tried for years not to admit that drugs was a problem in their particular sport — the governing bodies — were forced to accept the findings of the International Olympic Committee's Medical Commission.

The cycling bodies have fought drug-taking for over twenty years, and as a result have annually caught many cheats. But the sport has suffered internationally at the hands of the politicians, who instead of praising its enlightened actions have pointed to it as one of the worst for doping in the world.

It is worth noting that in both professional and amateur races throughout the world *every* major stage race and single-day classic race is automatically tested. The race leader (every day, even if he is the same rider) and the stage winner, and at least two at random, are obliged to report to the control as soon as the race ends. In a time-trial, the first four riders are tested. In cycling one rider from Denmark, Kim Andersen, has been disqualified for life for testing positive three times. He was reinstated this year.

Disqualification is the maximum punishment, and initially a person to win the competition four times if he wins in 1989. months — only enforced in the event of a second positive test — the loss of his victory and prize on the day he was tested, and being given last place plus a 10 minute time penalty if it is a stage race. In the case of the Tour de France, if the leader tested positive the time penalty would almost certainly cost him the race — equivalent to a fine of £130,000!

Many people, especially after the Olympic Games, are demanding that a cheat should be banned for life — but what if the sport is your life?

A professional sportsman, in cycling's case, races for money, and in so doing rides perhaps 30,000 miles a year. A cold, bronchitis (common in cycling), an accident or just a headache cannot be treated in the normal way, because everything prescribed by a general practitioner contains a proscribed substance. Lynford Christie was a lucky man when he was given the benefit of the doubt after giving a 'positive' test in the Olympics, as he surely knows — there have never been to my knowledge such lucky men in cycling.

In the eyes of many people, Pedro Delgado will not be seen as the winner of the Tour de France because he took a substance that would have been banned if it were used in the Olympic Games. As this substance — Probenicide — was not banned by the Union Cycliste Internationale, he was allowed to continue. Unfair? You have to make your own decision. Certainly Delgado suffered for a week during the race, as people called him a cheat.

His particular case was different. Someone from inside the medical unit used to test the riders leaked that Delgado's first test was 'positive'. That evening on Antenne 2 French television the presenter stunned the cycling world.

The second test was made in Paris, and before the result was announced officially Spanish television was reporting that Delgado's second test had proved negative. In fact, when the mistake was realized there was no need for the second test because the first should not have been leaked as positive.

Probencide is used to palliate dehydration and the build-up of uric acid, but the cynics were sure that it was also being employed because of its other property, which was to mask the use of steroids.

Two things come to mind: Delgado tested positive after winning the time-trial in the Alps, yet he knew that the first four riders to finish were automatically tested. He could have slowed on purpose and still won the Tour later.

Secondly, as the leader he was tested for the next ten days and all were negative tests, but whether he continued to use Probencide is not clear.

The positive test of Gert Theunisse is another strange case. The Dutchman was found to have used large amounts of the steroid testosterone and was duly penalized, losing all hope of the Tour.

Each day, he gave interviews (in tears!) saying he had taken nothing. The second test proved positive as well, but then an

Here is Shelly in a different rôle, feeding her 'charges' out on the route. Double Tour winner Laurent Fignon is in front.

eminent professor from a Dutch university said that he knew Theunisse very well and that it was possible to have a count of 20 in his body (an excessive amount) if the rider was making extreme efforts in hot conditions and in the mountains. The reply from a London test centre was 'Rubbish!'

The fight against drugs will go on, and we should all support it, yet, there are still too many anomalies to make one feel totally confident in the system.

The professional rider will spend a third of his life in the saddle in all weathers. A cold January and February is no excuse to stay indoors, because the body needs to accumulate the all-important basic 'miles' to build on when the season is under way. If a rider does not pedal himself into the new year he will become weaker, not stronger, as the season progresses, and drained to such an extent that he may not finish it at all.

It is not physical tiredness alone that causes most breakdowns, but the mental staleness of completing the same routine every day — facing his lonely seven hours' training session in all weathers.

Riders begin their stamina-building training in December, often with a friend or a local group of club amateurs, just to get the miles in. These rides are treated as pleasurable, and will rarely cover more than 80 miles in a single day, at a constant speed of 20–22 mph.

In January, after an early winter spent riding and interspersed with some gym work and skiing, the professional will join up with his team at a warm resort, such as the Côte d'Azur, to begin regular training and to meet his new team-mates. A new daily routine is soon established, although the riders will also devise an individual training schedule, aimed at bringing him to peak fitness for those races where he wants to excel. There are four targets in a rider's season: the spring classics, which are single-day races in France, Belgium, Holland and Italy between March and early May; the big tours, either of Italy or France — or both — between May and July; the world road-race championship in August; and the single-day classics that end the season in September and October. Only a handful of the greatest riders can expect to star in all these races.

The Tour de France figures highly as a target for all the world's best riders, so riders like Stephen Roche and Laurent Fignon will begin the year preparing for the event by riding early stage races such as Paris–Nice or Italy's Tirreno–Adriatico. They might also have a go at one or two of the single-day classics which cover distances similar in length to stages in the Tour. The month before the latter race is the time to put finishing touches to the weeks of basic preparation and racing, stepping up training to match the Tour distances and racing smaller stage races, such as the Tour of Switzerland in June.

André Darrigade made a habit of winning the first stage — he did it five times. But here on the Parc des Princes velodrome in 1958 his tour ended in tragedy, when he killed an official and suffered serious head injuries himself.

The riders aim to arrive at the start of the Tour de France in fine condition, perhaps having purposely increased their body fat content slightly to allow for the loss that will occur during the race. In this build-up period the rider will not have allowed himself to be ill, despite the extremes of weather during his training and racing. He will have kept his body in top condition by taking vitamin supplements, spending most of his spare time in bed, and receiving regular massage to clear away the lactic acid from his legs.

A rider's wife — who perhaps imagined she would be marrying into a glamorous way of life — will spend much of her time washing the endless supply of racing and training clothes and preparing the right diet, which will include a variety of good food with plenty of carbohydrates, no fat and little alcohol. Some riders, like Robert Millar, are vegetarian, but most eat veal or steak along with pasta. Yogurts and health foods are very popular, and endless bottles of water and mineral salt replacement drinks replace fluid lost during a day's racing. Drinking alcohol and smoking is rare among riders, even out of season. A professional rider's travelling kit will include a selection of miscellaneous items apart from his tools of the trade, such as spare shorts, track-mitts, white socks and racing jerseys. In his kit will be found embrocations and skin oils, toilet waters, creams for the inside of his shorts and his favourite novel! One of the main problems during a stage race is boredom in between racing and the arrival of the personal stereo has proved a boon, riders keeping collections of their favourite music by their bedsides. If he is in a foreign country for a long time, a newspaper in his own language is as welcome as a ten-pound note!

By the time the rider arrives at the start of the Tour he should feel very fit, mentally and physically, for the toughest three weeks of the season. He is not just expected to ride well — he also has to face the daily contact with the Press and television, for some riders more arduous than the race itself. During the Tour the competitors will get up early, perhaps six o'clock in the morning, to face a breakfast of steak and rice. Riders always eat their main food three hours before stage starts, but may also have a follow-up snack.

After the race there is possibly a dope control to visit if your number has been announced by the inspector; interviews with the Press (some riders disappear quickly if they have had a bad ride to avoid the journalists!); and the massage table to undergo. This is followed by dinner, during which the day's racing will be analysed, followed by a team talk about tactics for the next day's racing. This routine might not seem too bad for a while, but as the race goes on other problems can arise. Perhaps the daily multiple crashes have caused injury problems, or riders may have caught a cold, or during the hot

---

Perrier World Cup Race races 1989

18 March Milk—San Remo (It)

2 April Tour of Flanders (Belg)

9 April Paris—Roubaix (Fr)

16 April Liège—Bastogne—Liège (Belg)

22 April Amstel Gold Race (Holl)

30 July Wincanton International (GB)

6 August GP of the Americas (Can)

12 August San Sebastian—San Sebastian (Sp)

20 August Championship of Zurich (Switz)

17 September GP des Liberations (Team Time Trial) (Holl)

8 October Paris—Tours (Frl)

14 October Tour of Lombardy (It)

Other Major Races of the 1989 Season

February

7—12 Ruta del Sol (Sp)

9—12 Étoile de Bessèges (Fr)

15—20 Tour of the Mediterranean (Fr)

22—20 Tour of the Americas (USA)

March

1 GP Wielerrevue (Holl)

4 Het Volk (Belg)

5 Kuurne—Brussels—Kuurne (Belg)

5—11 Paris—Nice (Fr)

9—15 Tirreno—Adriatico (It)

April
5 Ghent—Wevelgem
12 Flèche Wallonne
24—15 May Tour of Spain

May
1 Henninger Turm (WG)
2—7 Four Days of Dunkirk (Fr)
9—14 Tour of Romandy (Switz)
21—11 June Tour of Italy
28—10 June Milk Race (GB)
29— 5 June Criterium Dauphiné—Libéré (Fr)

June
7—11 Tour of Luxembourg
12—18 GP Midi—Libre (Fr)
14—23 Tour of Switzerland
18 Tour of Philadelphia (USA)
25 National Road Championships (All countries)

July
1—23 Tour de France

August
8—13 Tour of Belgium
14—19 Tour of Holland
27 World road race championship (Fr)
29— 3 September Kellogg's Tour (GB)

September
3 GP Eddy Merckx (Belg)
9 Baracchi Trophy (It)
19—24 Étoile des Espoirs (Fr)
20 Paris—Brussels
24 GP des Nations (Fr)
27— 1 October Nissan Classic (Ire)

weather, a sunburn. I have seen riders cut the sleeves off their best shirts to put over their sunburnt arms. Worst of all, a rider may have had a bad day and lost time because of a crash, mechanical failure, sheer bad luck or bad judgment and missing a decisive attack. He will sit through his dinner in a state of low morale, and his team will talk to him all night if necessary to get him back into a mental state to go on next day.

There is also the problem of homesickness, and riders spend many hours on the telephone at night. They may receive bad news from home, as in the case of Pedro Delgado, who retired in tears on hearing of the death of his mother when lying fifth overall in 1986. Henni Kuiper, A Dutch rider who finished second in the 1977 and 1980 Tours, left the 1983 race when seventh overall after hearing that his father had had a serious accident.

As though the pressures of winning the race were not enough, the Tour riders are never out of the public's eye. The hotels of the teams are besieged by autograph-hunters, and this pursuit is made easier (although not intentionally) by the fact that the riders' room numbers are listed on boards in hotel foyers, and their keys left in the bedroom doors. This is to enable the team officials to come and go into the rooms as they please without disturbing the riders, who are often asleep at unusual times of day. In an attempt to satisfy the Press, and keep calls to his room at a minimum, the race leader will usually call a press conference during the race. There are few opportunities for this, so the rest day is favoured. Each Tour de France has only one day when there is no racing, and it is not usually welcomed by the riders. They fear their legs will stiffen up, so that even on the rest day some teams will go riding for 80 km.

At the end of any Tour, of 200 riders (the number can vary and there was a record 210 in 1986, but new rules now restrict the field size to 200) each one has a tale to tell of his experiences. Cyclists come in all shapes and sizes, and seem to have no average physique. However, all are slim when they start, and decidedly slimmer when they finish!

Here is an interesting comparison of the vital statistics of the three riders who won five times.

	Anquetil	Merckx	Hinault
Born	8.1.1934	17.6.1945	14.11.1954
Height	5' 8'''	6' 4"	5' 7"
Weight	11st 4lb	11st 7lb	9st 12lb
First Tour at	23	24	23
Last Tour at	32	31	31

Chapter 7
The Caravan

The Tour de France has its detractors, as does any event that has become the pinnacle of achievement in its sport. The riders complain that it is now too commercial, and that they get no consideration; others say the Tour has lost its direction in its search for the financial backers to keep it going.

Each has a point, but despite conflicting opinions on the Tour de France, one thing is agreed — it is the finest-organized event on the open roads.

On the day of the race itself the roads are closed to everybody except people carrying Tour identification passes, but despite this inconvenience the towns and cities welcome the Tour into their midst. If the event did not bring commercial and publicity value to the towns, cities and resorts through which it passes it would have ended years ago.

Wherever the race goes the disruption to everyday life is considerable, but in return the local hotels, bars, restaurants and shops have a field day. More than two thousand people arrive with the race, and many, many thousands more pass through as spectators. The Tour is seen as a travelling circus, its Big Top being the countryside itself, its arena the highways and its grandstands the towns and villages packed to capacity with spectators. Organizing an event on public roads involves travelling through city centres, complicated by one-way systems and narrow streets. The battle to obtain the permissions necessary to close busy centres and main linking arteries takes up much of the year. The police (with whom the Tour organization works closely) have to plan in minute detail how each town can carry on with a reasonably normal working day when half the roads are closed to traffic. The emergency services have to work out how they can reach fires or accidents occurring on the race route. When you think of the amount of planning and paperwork, it is easy to see why the Tour de France must be big and commercial, or die.

An exciting addition to the Tour caravan this year was a giant television screen which cost the organization two million francs. Despite the cost, it meant the spectators at the finish line could watch the race for two hours before the riders arrived.

Until 1987 the race had always been organized by journalists; Henri Desgrange, Victor and Jacques Goddet and Félix Levitan were all newspaper men. From the Second World War until he left in 1987, M. Levitan was the person mainly responsible for its development.

After M. Levitan's departure in the spring of 1987 the Société du Tour de France chose Jean-François Naquet-Radiguet as its new general manager but with less than a year's service he left and has been replaced by Jean-Pierre Courcel.

An annual turnover of £6,000,000 is needed to keep the race on the road, and a staff of forty-four people occupying the Société's headquarters on the fifth floor of a modern building at Issy-les-Moulineaux, near Paris, where it moved in 1987. The building also houses the sponsoring L'Équipe newspaper, the Presse Sports photographic agency and the Vélo cycling magazine, which in conjunction with the world professional body (FICP) is responsible for compiling the riders' world rankings.

The Société can be regarded as one part of the Tour Caravan. From these offices on the fifth floor its tentacles reach out across Europe during each year of deals and counter-deals.

Much of the backing for the race comes from the sponsors, but a major part of the income is derived from the publicity caravan that precedes the race by at least an hour, and which to many of the roadside spectators is the most interesting part!

The cost of placing a vehicle into the Tour Caravan is considerable, whether for a day or for the whole race. For example, a vehicle on the race for three weeks with a driver and two publicity girls could easily cost £60,000, so naturally companies who buy into the caravan make an intense effort to get a good return for their outlay.

Vehicles are specially designed and built to attract attention, and are often in the shape of the product being sold. One of the longest-standing supporters of the race is the Catch Company, which sells insect repellant. A fleet of red vehicles with giant models of dead flies and beetles on top brings home the message pretty clearly. The 'Caravane Publicitaire' was first seen in the 1930 race. This was also the Tour in which the organizers introduced the national teams for the first time.

Henri Desgrange was always concerned by the relations between riders and bicycle-manufacturers, which in his time were enjoying their halcyon days. He always suspected that this led to corruption, professionals being able to canvass among rival bicycle sponsors for the best deal. Riders often changed their sponsors during the season, especially if they had done well in the Tour, therefore increasing their market value to bicycle firms.

Desgrange's introduction of the publicity caravan, and at the same time of national teams instead of trade teams, reduced the advertising on the riders' jerseys and gave him the oppor-

Wherever the race goes the local hotels, bars, restaurants and shops have a field day.

The Catch Company have long been supporters of the Tour — and their fly-spray works!

tunity to sell space to the bicycle companies. It was not just bicycle companies, of course — anyone could take advantage of the thousands of spectators who stood waiting for the race. Beer and cigarette companies were a major source of income to the Tour, although nowadays France has banned such companies from using sporting events for their advertising.

The introduction of mobile advertising was a great success, and as the years passed companies tried harder to be the most attractive in the convoy, and to make their slogans stand out. The tyre company Michelin is still a caravan regular, with a replica of a pre-war fire engine and modern motor-bikes as mounts for their select group of Michelin Men. For most of the race route these skilful exhibitionists ride standing on the motor-bikes, steering with their bodies and waving to the crowd. They descend the mountains in similar fashion!

Cars balanced on two wheels — a caravan addition normally seen only when the race is in Belgium — pass by angled at 45 degrees, precariously hovering over a rider and passenger on a motorcycle combination, while other companies employ scantily clad girls to hand out chewing gum, chocolate and a variety of free gifts. By the time the riders race past, the spectators, decked in free paper hats and flags, look as though they have had a day out at the fair!

Because of the obvious dangers to unwary spectators, the Tour caravan is escorted by the gendarmerie, and is preceded by a police car bearing a flag saying *Caravane voiture pilote* (caravan pilot car). For some time afterwards the convoy drifts by until it arrives near the end of the stage, where it is gathered together for a grand passage over the finish line complete with a personal introduction by the Tour's 'Speaker', Daniel Mangeas.

The publicity caravan became greatly reduced in the 1960s and early 1970s, partly because sponsors put their money back into the trade teams, as this side of the professional sport again

The men on the Tour route enjoy seeing the pretty Coca-Cola girls.

Above: *The Colombia radio and television reporters never rest. The team from RCN have eight hours' air time a day to fill. What will they do if Luis Herrera ever wins the Tour?*

Left: *Riding skills of a different kind for the acrobats of the Tour Caravan.*

began to grow in interest. However, since the Tour's appeal has spread to riders outside Western Europe, companies involved in worldwide activities — such as Coca-Cola — have now become involved, committing themselves to the race to the tune of thousands of pounds. In recent years the caravan has been bigger than ever, with many of the sponsors (such as the daily Catch Sprints series) being given vehicles in the race convoy as part of the financial agreement.

The other 'caravan' which completes the Tour de France entourage is the thousand-strong press, radio and television corps, who keep the estimated 75 million viewers, listeners and readers informed as to the stories that abound during the heady month of July. Most events want — and need — media coverage to popularize them, but while many spend weeks saturating TV stations and newspaper offices with information in the hope of good coverage, the Tour is in the luxurious position of fending off those who want a place in the caravan. The increase in cars, motor-cycles, helicopters and equipment vans is adding to the annual problems of an already pressurized organization.

Some journalists have spent more than half their lives covering the race, and there is none more knowledgeable than Jacques Goddet himself, whose daily articles in *L'Équipe* have been read by millions over the last fifty years.

It is not easy to report the Tour de France accurately. Instead of a stadium or comfortable pressbox, there are just bumpy roads, hairpin bends and a race radio that does not always work, or give you the information exactly as you require it. It is now almost impossible to see the race first-hand, so journalists from all nationalities compare notes at the end of the day. The press facilities create many problems for the organizers. First of all there must be a building big enough to house up to five hundred people, which isn't always easy — for example, as when the race finishes on a mountain-top such as the Col du Tourmalet. In such cases a complete isolated village may be taken over. Other venues have included wine cellars (very popular with the journalists, even if cold!), hangars, churches, schools, town halls, and the restaurants of large corporations.

Modern technology presents another problem, and now that small computers have replaced typewriters journalists require power points, separate desks and quick access to phones to feed their stories directly to their newspaper's main computers.

> *There are just bumpy roads, hairpin bends and a race radio that does not always work.*

They're all pretty calm now, but wait until the riders appear! Photographers on the Tour have perhaps the most difficult task of all.

Claude and Philippe Sudres are the full-time Press Officers responsible for accrediting the journalists and for arranging the installation of telex and fax machines and the thirty telephones at every stage finish. They receive applications to follow the Tour all year round and they vet every applicant before putting him on the accepted list. Once a journalist has been accepted, the Sudres make sure every need is satisfied. The journalists — impatient when working towards their papers' deadlines — produce miles of copy within minutes of every stage finish, and expect detailed results of the racing within thirty minutes of the finish at the latest!

Radio reporters covering the race are an additional problem. They drive just ahead of the riders, giving their listeners an up-to-date report while whirling around the hairpin bends with

tyres squealing and clutches overheating. The Colombian radio team (which reports for two rival radio networks) takes every chance to go live to Bogotá, and be first with the news. I remember one Colombian reporter shouting down a coin-operated telephone kiosk in Provence, and before him the biggest pile of francs I've ever seen. The race had passed by in the meantime, but this did not slow down the reporter's tempo! The Colombians in action are a great source of entertainment, since they fill in as much as eight hours' air time a day reporting on the success of such riders as Luis Herrera and Fabio Parra. On one occasion a startled lady opened her front door and was almost run down by Colombian journalists trying to grab her phone. Afterwards they paid her handsomely before running back to the car to catch up with the race.

A busy press-room at the end of a stage of the Tour — for the journalists the day is just beginning.

The television crews also have a nerve-racking lifestyle, as cameramen from the host nation, or from Britain's Channel 4 and America's CBS (whose contract ended with the Tour last year) try to catch on film or video the significant moments that shape the race. The motorcycle-mounted cameramen pass a precarious day dangling from their mounts on some of the most dangerous roads in Europe. Still photographers also travel on motor-bikes, and perhaps because to a TV cameraman their photographs do not seem as urgent, the rivalry to get near a rider has at times developed into a major argument.

The television pictures are received at the finish line on a block of small monitors (television sets), where the commentators are ready to relay anywhere in the world. The pictures

Philippe Sudres, the Assistant Press Chief of the Tour.

reach the finish area from the cameraman, whose motor-cycle is specially equipped to transmit a signal up to a helicopter overhead, which bounces the signal on to the finish line.

The commentators see exactly the same picture as that being received in homes, but have the advantage of occasionally hearing Radio Tour in their 'cans' or headphones. The pictures are often dramatic, thanks to the great skills of the motor-cyclists.

Channel 4 has in the past four years developed the coverage of the Tour de France in Britain, and every evening transmits edited highlights of the same day's stage. This was a major step forward for cycling on British television, which beforehand had been restricted to weekend compilations by London Weekend Television's Saturday afternoon *World of Sport* programme. The late David Saunders, television's first cycling commentator, and London Weekend executive John Bromley introduced the Tour to British television. Now on Channel 4 the introduction of daily coverage of the race has seen audiences increase from 300,000 a day to a record of 3.1 million on the final day of last year's race.

Adrian Metcalfe, until recently Channel 4's commissioning Editor for Sport, was the man responsible for taking the gamble, and he followed an encouraging first year by appointing the production company Television Sport and Leisure (run by ex-BBC *Grandstand* editors Mike Murphy and Brian Venner), to improve the production. Mike and Brian, who have covered most sports, suffer from the same disease that has kept journalists covering the Tour for fifty years — having seen the event, they have an unstoppable urge to tell everyone about it. It is hoped that the ideas gained from the experiences of the past two years this summer will be further developed when the race is again given major exposure on Channel 4 television.

The CBS network, which covered the event exclusively for America for five years until ABC television won the contract for this year, was almost a family of its own with between thirty and thirty-five engineers, commentators, cameramen and outside broadcast editors setting up a complete mobile home alongside the event. Cycling has attracted more interest in the United States since the American team won nine gold medals in the Olympic Games in Los Angeles in 1984, and since Greg LeMond made history by winning the Tour in 1986.

The CBS presentation was tailored for a special audience which had little or no understanding of the complexities of cycling. This prompted the CBS team to make a production (shown weekly throughout the Tour on Saturdays and Sundays) which was less a sports report than a drama. The team's 'commander' was executive producer David Michaels, a Californian who prepared for his 24-hour-days (he hardly even found time to go to bed) covering the race by looking after his garden at Christmas-time in a warm West Coast climate!

Michaels, with his producers Victor Frank and Rick Gentile, led his 'army' into battle using four cars, a helicopter and three motor-bikes. The support team was entirely committed to featuring every last story of a given day. Sleep and food took a very poor second place to this, and every Sunday evening the completed programme was sent by satellite to New York for immediate transmission into American homes. When the company's contract ended last year the Tour organizers took the unprecedented step at the end in Paris of issuing a press release thanking the CBS team for helping the race obtain a worldwide reputation. The team itself won three television 'Emmys' for their programmes.

The French television facilities unit, SFP, are responsible for producing the host nation's pictures for use by all the TV networks on the Tour, and they have a difficult job every day of the race. SFP have the logistical problem of moving the television tribunes — banks of TV monitors and miles of cabling — every day to a new site which can be 250 miles away. Many of the juggernaut-size trucks are obliged to cross mountain passes through the night, and, because of their size they have to stop at every hairpin bend on the climbs and descents, reverse and have another go at getting round!

The setting up of the finish area on any stage is usually completed by midday, and then the complete SFP crew pull out long tables, put out the wine and barbecue their lunch. The motor-cycle crews and cameramen have already left to find a

Luis Herrera lives at altitude in Bogotá, so it is not surprising that he loves climbing in the Tour. The television cameraman catches all the action for the commentators working at the finish line.

In 1989 the Tour expects:
To employ — 220 temporary staff.
To use — 1,495 vehicles.
To host — 3,750 people following the race every day.
To rely on — 13,000 policemen to secure the route.
To be escorted by — 35 police motor-cyclists.

The real drama — the dramatic fightback by Stephen Roche — was not seen until the last hundred yards.

restaurant approximately fifty kilometres back along the route, ready to pick up the race later in the afternoon.

The CBS team had its own mobile home which drove until 3 a.m. every day to be in position for the finish. Once there Penny and Mike Mallinson — whose London-based Translux company is accustomed to working on film shoots with top stars — spent the day wrestling on windy mountain summits with the sun-blinds and preparing sandwiches for the worn-out team who invaded the home at 5 p.m. every evening.

When the Tour arrives at any town or mountain finish the cafés or restaurants take a considerable amount of money, but they will earn every penny. The patron, who has probably only a few staff and his family, is well aware of the speed with which food will be required before the race arrives. I have seen many a journalist co-opted to the kitchen to prepare the Salade de Tomate and to slice bread in order to keep things on the move.

In recent years the SFP has improved its coverage by bringing pictures of the morning mountain crossings back to the finish line by helicopter. Pilots land on precarious plateaux and collect video cassettes from camera teams, then fly them back so that they may be played into the opening of the day's programme.

Of course, things do go wrong. If, for example, there is low cloud on the mountains — which is not unusual — and the helicopters are not able to fly, there will not be any pictures until the riders approach the finishing line. The two motor-cycles which are usually placed with the leader(s) and with the chaser(s) do not always give the commentators (or the viewers) the pictures they would most like to see. This was highlighted in 1987 at La Plagne when one camera followed Laurent Fignon, the stage winner, and the second covered the chase by race leader Pedro Delgado. The real drama, though, was the dramatic fightback by Stephen Roche, lying second overall, who was not seen until the last hundred yards! At Blagnac, near Toulouse, the transmission became a nightmare for the commentators when torrential rain (which burst sewer systems in a few minutes) wiped out all the commentary positions as water poured in.

Embarrassingly, pictures away from the finish were perfect, so the Channel 4 viewers were obliged to listen to a telephoned commentary from a rambling commentator who had no idea what was going on! It was the hardest job in my Tour experience so far!

Chapter 8
Tactics and Equipment

Although there can be no doubt about the athletic achievements involved simply in *finishing* the 2,500-mile race, at the end of the day the Tour de France is intrinsically a thriving business, and one should remember that, as professionals, the riders take part to earn their living. Like all successful businessmen, they have learned their trade well, but the most proficient earn the most money.

Because the Tour is now a very commercial concern, it would be difficult — some say impossible — to revert to the national teams formula last used in 1968, where riders represented their country. This system is always under consideration by the race organizers, but they face great difficulties from trade team riders who race together every day of the season but would become rivals during July when they represented their country. This situation does exist in the world road-race championship each summer, and trained eyes can see — but never prove — riders from different countries helping one another to win, because the very next day they will be team-mates again!

National pride takes second place with professional riders — first place goes to the companies who pay their salaries.

This is the reason that national pride takes second place with professional riders — first place goes to the companies who pay their salaries. The team sponsors expect good exposure for their annual outlay, which is often in excess of £2,000,000. The only acceptable formula for the Tour de France in the present commercial climate is to invite the trade teams.

A rider's earnings come from many sources, and because the average career of a professional cyclist is said to be only eight years, he will naturally seek his money in as many directions as possible.

Firstly, there is the contract with a main team sponsor, which is usually signed for one or two years. This contract fee can vary from a few thousand pounds a year, plus equipment, to more than half a million. A successful rider can boost his earnings by agreeing clauses in his contract which specify bonus payments for outstanding achievement. This may include stage wins or major victories such as the world championship, the Tour de France, or the Tour of Italy. Of course, he will also get prizes from the races, although in the Tour de France an overall winner usually gives most of his share of the prize money to the other riders in the team — the victory alone will give him financial security. He will be able to negotiate a higher basic salary, and also to increase his earnings from product licensing and personal appearances. Nowadays a rider winning the Tour de France can expect to become a millionaire. The other team members — the *domestiques* — will have more than contributed to the success of an individual rider, and earned their share of the prize money.

In these modern days of split-second timing, ultra-light equipment, and back-up teams who can change wheels in less than nine seconds, no rider would be able to win the Tour without the support of a strong team. During all stages of the race the *domestiques* will try to make sure their talented leader can use his abilities to the full when the opportunity comes. If he punctures, they will wait while the mechanic changes his wheel, and then pace him back to the main field, saving him from wasting valuable energy. (A rider hidden in the slipstream of others is sucked along, saving at least a third of his energy.) If the leader falls and breaks his bike a *domestique* will give him his own machine. In stage races, a rider of similar size to the leader rides close to him for as long as he can, ready to sacrifice his own bike in the event of problems.

On hot days the *domestiques* are kept busy collecting drinks from the team cars following to take back to their leaders. Because everyone knows they do not have the ability to win the race, *domestiques* will not be challenged, whereas if the leader himself dropped back for a drink he would run the risk of being attacked by other team leaders.

Tactics are the most vital part of any stage race, the ability to 'read' the race is crucial — an attack at the wrong time, for example, could waste vital energy which might be needed later to counter a potential winning attack.

Every rider knows his own strengths and weaknesses, and because the professionals compete against each other frequently in races throughout the season, he also knows the other riders' shortcomings. If, for example, a rider is a fast sprinter who loves the elbow-to-elbow tussle of a stage finish,

Teamwork is vitally important in the Tour and riders always call upon their team-mates for help. Here the Belgian ADR team make sure their leader, Eddy Planckaert (green jersey) is kept in a good position for the sprint finishes.

Barry Hoban keeps cool in the midday sun in Avignon — what better than a cabbage leaf under his hat?

Thankfully, there are always the gamblers who throw caution to the wind.

and ends up winning by the width of his tyre, the tactic to beat him would be to make sure that the race did not end in a massed sprint, so the teams will try to help one of their riders break clear. This is one reason why, near the end of a stage, the speed is higher. Another reason is that the teams with the sprinters are trying to keep the pace high to make it impossible for anyone to get ahead. This is the type of finish that sometimes ends in a *domestique* achieving the stage victory that will make him famous!

These days, because of the aggression shown by many teams out to win stages, very few races have ended in a massed sprint for the line. Of course, if you want to win the Tour overall the object is always to gain time over your rivals.

If, like Hinault and Anquetil, a rider's strength lies in the time-trial, the other potential winners will turn to different methods to beat their rivals. One method might be to use the high mountains to gain more time than they expect to lose during the time-trial.

Lucien Van Impe and Federico Bahamontes, the Tour's great climbers, were the masterly exponents of this last tactic, and although both won the King of the Mountains title six times, they also each won the Tour once. Hinault and Anquetil, in contrast, would have responded by trying to limit their losses in the mountains, hoping to recover in the time-trials the time lost.

Riders who feel they are in with a chance of winning the overall race will study the complete course for months beforehand. They will note the placing of the time-trials, their distance and the nature of the terrain, and they will study the mountains and how they fall into the race route. On some stages the finish may be in the mountains; on others where the mountains are placed early in a day's route an attack would be foolhardy, as the long, flat roads to the finish would allow the opportunity for the rest to catch up.

Thankfully, there are always the gamblers who throw caution to the wind and break clear from the start, with no obvious thought other than to be first to the finish. It is men like these who give the races their colour.

During the build-up races before the Tour de France the team leader will assess his personal chance of victory, and will then select his team for the race from a squad of perhaps twenty riders. This will be done in consultation with his Directeur Sportif (team manager). He will decide which of them can be of most help to him during the Tour. He will choose eight or nine team-mates, depending on the size of the team being accepted by the race. Teams that enter do not always expect to win the Tour — they are too realistic for that — so may simply put in a team of men capable of winning a few stages, and perhaps the green points jersey as well. This happened in 1987 and 1988, when the Dutch Super Confex squad won many stages and the green jersey (in 1987). In Holland the team has received a great amount of publicity, achieving the sponsor's aim.

Then there are the low-budget teams which do not have their superstar, like the British team in 1987. These teams take part to learn, and only dream of success. Nowadays, because of the importance of the team time-trial stage, any teams hoping for victory must be strong as a unit if their leader is not to lose time on this special stage.

The TTT is always held by the third day of the race (in 1988 it was on the first day), otherwise the organizers risk upsetting the balance of teams as they lose riders who retire, and which would leave a team leader with no team to help him.

In general, the leaders do not like the team time-trial because it means they are not in complete charge of their own destiny. Unlike the individual time-trial, the team races together over the course, and the time for the stage is taken from the fifth rider of the team to cross the line. This means that there is no point in the leader going ahead on his own, or even with one strong rider, because his time will always be the same as the fifth man to finish. Sometimes a team will sacrifice a strong time-triallist by asking him to keep a high pace as long as possible, then he will drop off exhausted near the end.

The French Système U team fight to keep their leader Laurent Fignon (second from back) *in contention overall in the team time-trial in 1986.*

In this way a nine-man team may come home with just five men, with the rest being left to struggle on, making sure that they beat the day's time limit. The best teams (those with the high budget that has enabled very strong riders to be drawn into one squad) do particularly well in the team time-trial and they share the pace-making, finishing together. Only riders who fall or have mechanical trouble are left behind. Very often the winners of the team time-trial occupy all the leading places overall for a few days as happened in 1988.

As a general principle, the team leaders tend to watch each other, responding to one another's attacks, while the *domestiques* are given the job of following the rest. The leaders are easy to spot, as their race numbers usually end in 1. For example, in 1987 Stephen Roche was number 11 and Pedro Delgado, 51 and last year Delgado was 171. The previous year's winner (should he ride) is always given number 1. As the race progresses, and the overall classification projects the contenders at or near the top, *domestiques* will be seen at the starts each morning with numbers inked on to their hands or on a scrap of paper taped to their handlebars. Their job for the day is to watch the progress of these riders and if they attack, to try to go with them — a lot easier said than done!

A team-mate in a breakaway group is constantly advised of tactics to employ by the team's Directeur Sportif, who will come alongside in a car. If the group is gaining too much time (endangering his team leader's time advantage overall), the rider will be instructed not to help the attack gain any more ground. Instead he will be told to ride at the back, rest and think of winning the stage. When this happens the other riders might also change their tactics and stop working to prevent giving the man at the back an easy ride to the line.

During the three weeks the Tour de France is on the road the riders will save their effort until the terrain or race pattern

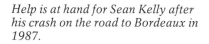

Help is at hand for Sean Kelly after his crash on the road to Bordeaux in 1987.

presents an opportunity. Otherwise, especially in the flatter stages, they concentrate on losing no time to the men they fear. They won't take much part in the in-fighting between teams looking for a stage win, or perhaps an early capture of the yellow jersey.

Tactics go wrong, of course, otherwise the race would be no fun!

In 1956 the Frenchman Roger Walkowiak — who had never won a major race, and was therefore not marked by the race favourites — gained half an hour during a two-day period over the expected contenders. They thought they would recover the lost time, but he defended enough of his gains — by marking the top riders — to win in Paris. Walkowiak never won a major race again during his nine-year career, and although he won the 1956 Tour, just look at his other placings in the race: 1951 — fifty-seventh; 1953 — forty-seventh; 1955 — did not finish; 1957 — did not finish; 1958 — seventy-fifth.

Look closely at this picture, because at first it appears the team manager is giving Alex Stieda of Canada a drink. In fact he is making full use of the opportunity to pull the rider up the hill — note Stieda's grip on the bottle.

Riders carry a small detailed route in their pocket, showing the distances between towns and the heights of the mountains. The signs at the entry to the towns help the riders to see how far to go and what terrain lies ahead.

On the long stages the 'convicts of the road' (as they have been known since the very early Tours) pedal at gentle speeds of less than 20 mph, since the leaders are not interested in attacking on an eight-hour ride over a flat course. But the smaller teams might send riders ahead in the hope they will survive to win the day's prizes. However, the flatter stages can be interesting, especially if the weather is bad or the roads — as in Northern France or Belgium — are surfaced with cobblestones big enough to break the bikes.

Above: *Wind direction causes the riders to form an echelon pattern on the road so that only the leader of the line feels the full force of the wind. The other riders in the line are either being blown backwards by the wind or moving forward in the shelter of the rider in front, both motions saving energy until it is this rider's turn at the front.*

In such conditions the leaders are vigilant and (especially in crosswinds) keep up a fast tempo, forcing the bunch to fragment into diagonal patterns, called echelons. The drawings show how riders move in an echelon, each spending a brief moment at the front in the wind before allowing it to blow them backward along the line and into the recovery area behind the riders moving forward.

This is a simple tactic of progression, but only the strongest riders survive the pace in the leading echelon. Others will form their own, perhaps a few yards behind and so on. If the pressure stays on at the front, gaps between the groups open until the leading group goes ahead, gaining many minutes. The atmosphere in the echelon is not always convivial either! The riders keep their formation tight, with arms brushing the legs of others as they pass up and down the line. Signs of weakness are quickly spotted by members of other teams, and the rider will be 'shut out' of the circular movement and be blown away to the group behind. If he does not go, or tries to shelter at the back of the echelon, it is not unusual to see him climbing out of a ditch after a touch of wheels!

Only when the leaders are reduced to two or three in the overall classification does it become easier to concentrate on competing in straight shows of strength.

Most sports throughout the world are won and lost on skill, but in cycle-racing tactics are paramount, and even then equipment can still have the final say.

For almost a century, bicycles have remained faithful to the diamond-shaped frame, but during the 1980s technical developments aimed at producing better performances in time-trials resulted in a strange new breed of custom-built bicycles. Every year new bicycle shapes — still based, however, on the diamond frame — appear, and most teams have a separate set of 'low-profile' streamlined machines for the time-trials. These are all designed to reduce 'drag' through the air. Every team seems to have its own special version: some have a smaller front wheel, a sloping top tube, or pear-shaped frame tubing for the conventional round. Handlebars can be straight instead of being dropped, and instead of spoked wheels, disc wheels are used to cut down wind turbulence — these wheels use carbon fibre sheeting to connect the rim to the hub, and can cost up to £2,000 each. Riders say disc wheels can help them improve by as much as five seconds a mile. These wheels are not allowed in the bunched races (except team time-trials) because they are difficult to manœuvre and as they are solid they catch any crosswinds.

Bicycles used in road races and mountain stages are slightly heavier than time-trial bikes, perhaps 22lb to 16lb, but a light bike would react unfavourably in winds or during descents at speeds up to 65 mph. On both bikes *dérailleur* gears give a selection of fourteen different pedalling speeds. A wrong gear chosen on a climb or in a time-trial could cost the rider the race.

Riders always choose a gear on which they feel comfortable. If they are attacking or sprinting they will use a higher gear, which means the resistance against the pedals is greater but the distance travelled for each pedal revolution is farther.

Above: *The £3,000 ultra-light machine for time-trialling awaits in the start-house for its rider to mount it for the individual test. His shaved legs are just visible!*

Left: *No, Greg LeMond's bike isn't bending under the strain! The American is employing all the latest innovations for the individual time-trial on his way to overall victory in 1986.*

Bad luck for Malcolm Elliott, who waits for his service car and a new back wheel. Ahead lies a hard chase to regain the field.

Most tyres are tubular in design with the inner tube sewn inside the outer tube, which has the tread on it. These tyres, weighing only five or six ounces, are made from either cotton or silk. Silk tubular tyres are slightly lighter, but are not as durable, and are more prone to puncture. These are normally used only in time-trials, where the emphasis on speed means the equipment is scant and as light as possible.

The tyres are stuck on to the rim with shellac — a compound which sets to a rock-hard finish, holding the tubular tyre in place — and although wheels are changed in the event of a puncture by the team's mechanic, if a rider falls too far behind the team manager passes him a spare tyre and leaves him! If he punctures after this happens, he will have to rip off the old tyre and replace it himself.

The clothing worn by racing cyclists has always been both functional and fashionable when compared to other sports. More recently the varied colours and designs of cycling clothes have been adapted for general purposes. Pop groups, for example, have often appeared wearing shorts and racing jerseys on stage.

Racing clothing is generally tight-fitting for comfort, and with the aim of creating as little wind resistance as possible. The shorts have a comfortable chamois insert and are skin-tight, while racing jerseys also hug the contours of the body.

Shoes are made from a soft leather upper with a man-made base, usually plastic, which is perforated to allow water to drain out and the feet to stay cool. Like ski boots, cycling shoes are vitally important and are made purely for riding. Underneath the shoes there is fitted a form of clamp that fits on to the pedal to lock the foot in place. Another method is to use a shoe plate with a slot in it. This is screwed to the base of the shoe, which slots on to the pedal. The shoe can then be strapped tight, so that the rider can both push and pull when climbing. Should he fall, a quick-release system saves him from sliding along the road with the bike! Fingerless gloves — track-mitts — reduce the blisters which form when a rider has been climbing for a couple of hours, or has been gripping the handlebars over bad roads.

As riders are in constant fear of catching cold, they always wrap up in warm clothing before and after racing. In the mountains the spectators wait at the summits to hand out newspapers. These are not for reading during the half-hour it may take a rider to descend to the valley, but for stuffing up the front of the jersey to keep out the wind! Survival to fight another day has always been the first thought in the mind of a *coureur* in the Tour de France!

Chapter 9
The Tour Féminin

Since 1985 the Tour Féminin has been the Longo and Canins show, but the 1988 edition — the 5th since its inception in 1984 — may prove to have been the final curtain call of the world's top two stage-race riders.

As happened with the men's Tour in its formative years, the women have struggled to find their own identity, and the possession of two dominant riders like Jeannie Longo and Maria Canins has, strangely, not helped to create an interesting event. After the 1988 race there were rumours that this would be the last, or that the Tour Féminin at best would move to a new date and away from the obvious comparisons made with the longer men's marathon.

Since 1985 the Tour Féminin has been the Longo and Canins show . . .

But the organizers have decided to change nothing this year 'for the benefit of women's cycling'. It could turn out to be the best race ever, too, as Longo may not ride and Canins is showing her age.

Until the mid-1970s, the Tour de France was almost entirely male-dominated. Although women were allowed in the advanced caravan (where pretty girls and shapely figures were deployed to help the public remember the products advertised) they were not seen in the zone known as the 'echelon course' — the actual racing area between the leading police outriders and the broom wagon behind the last man.

I wonder what would Desgrange have thought when, eighty years on, the organization recognized the increased interest in women's racing and put on the first Tour Féminin? A whole bunch of women in their own Grande Boucle!

The first race, between 30 June and 22 July 1984, was an experiment in every way. Women's racing was not something new — they had had their world championships since 1958 — but so far it had evoked little interest. It had not been thought necessary to formulate world stage-racing rules in the same precise detail as had been done for the men. The organizers had therefore followed the amateur rules, and had begun with a race of 1,051 km — as far as an amateur men's race, but spread over the whole month of the professional Tour de France, instead of the usual twelve days (the normal period for an amateur national tour). At first (just as in the early men's Tour) the women did not rush to take part in the Tour Féminin, and only thirty-six riders lined up at the start in Bobigny, outside Paris. Of these, thirty-five returned to finish on the Champs-Élysées. The organizers blamed the Los Angeles Olympic Games (which for the first time included a women's road race championship) for keeping away the best riders.

With such a small field, the spectacle would have lost all impact if many of the girls had abandoned the race part-way through, so the organization decided to relax the daily time limits, letting it be discreetly known that they wanted all the riders to finish in Paris. Sadly, the only one who did not was

Britain's Helen Parritt, who crashed and broke her collar-bone on the second day of the Tour.

The Tour Féminin is a much shorter version of the men's route, and starts each day at a town about two hours' ride from the finish line used for both races. This makes it very tiring for the officials and back-up teams, who face daily early evening drives of up to three hundred kilometres to reposition themselves ahead of the men's race. But this situation will not change as long as the race continues to run concurrently with the men's event.

The women's event has added a new dimension to the Tour de France; it has extended the day's spectacle for roadside spectators, and has given extra advertising opportunities to the sponsors. It is in fact financed by the sponsorship proceeds from the men's tour.

The first Tour Féminin had eighteen stages broken by five rest days, but most of the 'rest' days had to be spent in travelling, to keep up with the men's 4,000-km race. Although the daily distances were short by the men's standards, the gradients of the mountains such as La Plagne (6,463 ft) and the Col de Joux-Plane (5,620) were just the same!

Most of the stages in this first event were flat and, perhaps not surprisingly, the Dutch riders swept up the daily sprint finishes. Mieke Havik won five stages, and her team a total of fifteen! In stage racing, however, winning sprints may give you a day's success, but rarely overall victory. The reason is that all the field is given the same time, except that the first three are occasionally granted small time bonuses of a few seconds. Riders make the real time gains over one another in the mountains, or in individual time-trials.

The women may not race as far as the men, but the mountains are just as steep. Here on the Puy de Dôme two Chinese girls struggle to the end of another stage.

*Marianne Martin, an American who
wasn't even considered for the
American Olympic team in 1984,
was an outstanding winner of the
first Tour Féminin.*

It was in fact in the mountains during the latter half of the race that the American Marianne Martin, with her neatly cut shoulder-length red hair, surprised everybody as she danced on the pedals to gain enough time to win both the race and the title of Queen of the Mountains. But although Marianne's victory was as convincing as any later achieved, she was little known in her own country and was not even considered for the Olympic Games. She hasn't ridden in the Tour Féminin since.

This first race was greeted with mixed feelings. The Press, who for many years had concerned themselves solely with male cycling, chose to ignore it almost completely. Only the Dutch journalists showed substantial interest in reporting it, but for obvious reasons — they were winning most of the stages! The helpers co-opted to the women's race by the Tour organization would have preferred to be working on the more prestigious men's event but as the race progressed they changed their opinions when they saw how the women coped with the stresses and injuries of a long race.

The Tour Féminin developed a separate identity. Although the girls were rivals in the race they became close friends outside it, and even helped each other with spare equipment. Everybody, it seemed, wanted everybody else to finish. And they did.

As the French said after the first Tour: 'Bien joué, Mesdames!' The interest in women's stage racing attracted the attention of the world governing body (FIAC), who rushed in rules that forced organizers to reduce the daily distances during stage races, and allow a maximum period for any promotion to be spread over no more than twelve racing days. The new rules — announced in November 1984 – gave the Tour Féminin organizers major problems for the second race the following July (1985), as plans were already well advanced. It was too late to reorganize the Tour in order to conform to the new regulations, so the Tour Féminin was virtually split on this occasion into two separate events. The first of these was a twelve-day race from La Gacilly in Brittany to St Étienne and the second was a five-day affair from Laguepie, north of Toulouse, to the Champs-Élysées.

There was a day's gap between the two races, and the teams finishing the first had the choice of going home or continuing. Of course, everyone stayed for the second event — as the organizers had expected — and the riders hardly noticed any changes at all. The colours of the leaders' jerseys were different for the second event, the race leader's jersey being violet instead of yellow, while the points jersey was white instead of green.

In order that there should be one overall victor in Paris, a competition aggregated the two races to find the winner of the Challenge Tour de France, for which a yellow jersey was awarded on the Champs-Élysées. The organizers had found a way around the new rules. The yellow jersey for overall winner of the two races was finally awarded to the Italian Maria Canins, and the green points jersey to France's Jeannie Longo.

If FIAC had postponed the new rules until the following year, 1986, allowing the organizers to continue with arrangements already agreed in 1985, none of these complications would have been necessary. In many ways it was fortunate that the Italian wonder woman Maria Canins and France's own super-star Jeannie Longo were so far ahead of the field in ability that they finished first and second in both races, which kept the same result in the final analysis. The Press found the points system too complicated to explain, which gave them yet another reason to ignore the event.

Since 1985, the Tour Féminin has been a duel between two women. Maria Canins (left) has won twice. In 1988 Jeannie Longo scored the equalizer! Now it is two wins each in the last four Tours, and 1989 may see Canins go one up if Longo retires.

In 1985, the Tour Féminin opened its twelve-day 'first' race with a Prologue time-trial in Lannester over a 2.5-km course. This individual test gave Henny Top, a Dutch policewoman, the first yellow jersey, hinting immediately at another Dutch procession of stage winners, as in the previous year. But the quality of the race entry was much better than in 1984, and there were seventy-two entrants, including Britain's 1982 world champion Mandy Jones, who opened well by finishing sixth in the time-trial. Mandy was dogged by a calf muscle injury, but nevertheless remained a real challenger until eventually forced to retire in the Alps. She underwent successful surgery in England later, and although she has never raced again as an international, she has won a number of British time-trial titles. Meanwhile Maria Canins, now forty and the holder of a dozen national cross-country skiing titles, discovered that her new-found love of cycling could be equally rewarding. In this second Tour Maria — determined to win — took the lead off Jeannie Longo on the 48-km mountainous eighth stage from Chatel — where the race started with a five-mile high-speed descent — to the ski station of Avoriaz above Morzine in the Alps. Longo finished second, losing almost three minutes. Signora Canins struck again in the 22-km individual time-trial between Corrençon en Vercors and St Nizier de Moucherotte, where the undulating course again favoured the strong Italian lady.

It was generally agreed that this 1985 race was already much harder than the first Tour Féminin, and Maria Canins ended the first 'part' for the overall Challenge Tour de France with a lead of 13 minutes 14 seconds over Longo.

The Press, confused by the two-race system, continued to report the event as a seventeen-day single Tour.

The 'second' race was only five days to Paris and produced little change, although there was almost a grand finale for Britain when Catherine Swinnerton broke clear of the field on the Champs-Élysées, together with France's Dominique Damiani. The French girl gambled that the field (who were only seconds behind) would not catch them, and she refused to help Catherine set the pace. Poor Catherine had done too much pace-making to win the sprint, which was a formality for Damiani. The Stoke girl's second place remains Britain's best.

In 1986 the third Tour Féminin was organized under the new rules which had emanated from the world body. These laid down that there should be one race, over 996 km. It continued to run concurrently with the men's Tour, but because of the shorter race period it started a week later. By the time the men passed through the women's start town at Granville they had been on the road a week. There were fifteen stages, a Prologue time-trial and three rest days, the latter again used to travel by car to keep up with the longer men's event. Maria Canins,

The stages may be shorter for the women — but the mountains are just as steep. But whatever the terrain, Jeanne Longo and Maria Canins (in yellow) have been inseparable for three years.

Just like in the men's event, the girls also finish in the Champs-Élysées. Here, Maria Blower (nearest the camera), finishes her first Tour in twenty-second place.

thirty-seven, was again facing the world's most improving woman rider, the new world champion Jeannie Longo, now Mrs Ciprelli.

In this third Tour Canins opened with a win in the Prologue, but Longo fired back with victory in the next day's road race from Granville to Saint-Hilaire-du-Harcouët. But this was just shadow-boxing — both knew that the real showdown would again be in the mountains.

By now the Press had at last realized that the Tour Féminin was not going to go away and were taking notice — some were even following it during the day! Television was giving a five-minute résumé each evening, and of course the Italian television network RAI was having a field day, thanks to Maria. The Italian men, as expected, were not doing as well in their event, with the exception of bunch-sprint specialist Guido Bontempi.

Once again the high mountain peaks decided the overall winner. Canins won the stage over the Col d'Aspin (4,885 ft) and the Col de Peyresourde (5,152) to Luchon, and then four days later delivered the coup de grâce in the Alps during the nightmare 69-km stage from Guillestre to the top of the Col du Granon. The finishing climb up the Granon is twelve miles of narrow, unforgiving road. Without doubt it was the cruellest addition to the race.

Canins was a clear victor, but she was a specialist climber. She left behind her a trail of devastation, as distraught girls zig-zagged from side to side on the narrow road, some crying with the pain and others calling out for a push.

It is not unknown for the men to ask for assistance when they are in difficulty in the mountains — and they pay the fines happily if they are caught. But these girls were receiving help from every quarter; even gendarmes on motor-bikes were leaning over, giving them a helping hand — no one, it seemed,

These girls were receiving help from every quarter.

Britain's most consistent competitor in the Tour Féminin has been Clare Greenwood. She finished seventh in 1984, and has also finished eighteenth and twenty-fourth.

could just stand by and watch the suffering. One British competitor said afterwards: 'I looked back to see the whole Belgian team holding on to their team car. I was passed by an 11-stone Dutch sprinter being passed from hand to hand by Dutch spectators. In the end I screamed for them to push me as well.'

This rather farcical situation (which did not affect the two leaders, but certainly altered the lower part of the overall classification) brought a promise from the organizers that the rules would be properly applied in 1987 and that time limits would be observed.

The 1987 race was without question the best of the first four. It began well for twice runner-up Jeannie Longo, who won the opening Prologue time-trial at Sable-sur-Sarthe by just five seconds from Maria Canins, the overall winner for the past two years. The Grenobloise was the first to receive the leader's yellow jersey, and a continuance of the annual Franco-Italian battle was assured.

Eighty-five riders, from fourteen nations, made the best entry yet, with the Soviet Union entering a team for the first time. The Press were certainly in a more appreciative mood, although the predictable contest between Longo and Canins was not always conducive to imaginative writing. Now, however, after three years, there were also fresh names among the girls, these being led by the Soviet newcomers.

Tamara Poliakova, a blonde rider able to speak English, won three stages, finishing fourth overall, while the Dutch sprinters were losing stages rather than winning. West Germany's Viola Paulitz and Jutta Niehaus also enjoyed stage successes, but overall it remained a two-girl race.

Another British Tour regular is Sue Thompson, who recently married professional cyclist Alan Gornall. As Sue Thompson, she has ridden the Tour for the last three years.

Longo desperately wanted to win the Tour Féminin, and she had spent her pre-season training in the nearby Alps building herself up — and slimming down — for a real attempt at beating the Italian climbing specialist.

She had achieved almost everything else in the sport. She was the world road-race champion for a second year, the pursuit world champion on the track, and she had also set a record distance for the women's hour record, both indoor and out. The Tour Féminin would complete the set.

She had made a good start in the Prologue, but it was not maintained and she lost her lead two days later at Futuroscope, near Poitiers, to Monique Knol from Holland, the stage winner.

There was another unexpected change in the lead the next day from Linards to Chaumeil, where Roberta Bonanomi became the surprise new wearer of the yel-

Before the men arrive in Paris, the Tour Féminin completes its final stage over the last course on the Champs-Élysées.

Results So Far
1984:
1,051 km
1. Marianne Martin (USA) 29 hr 39 min 25 sec; 2. H. Hage (Hol) at 3–17; 3. D. Schumway (USA) at 11–51; 4. V. Simmonet (F) at 12–13; 5. C. Lutz (F) at 13–22; 6. B. Wise-Steffan (USA) at 13–47.
British: 7. Clare Greenwood at 14–44; 19. Judith Painter at 24–45; 27. Pauline Strong at 33–53; 31. Helen Edwards at 41–20; 3. Louise Garbutt at 44–57.
Points: Mieke Havik (Hol).
Mountains: Marianne Martin
Team: USA.

low jersey in the Italian team. The stage had been marred by an early crash that took out Canada's Denise Kelly and the Swiss Manuela Wohlgemuth, while in the gaps that formed in the field many others lost time. Significantly, Canins finished 28 seconds ahead of Longo, although both had been left behind by an inspired Bonanomi.

Two days later there was another major surprise when Longo rid herself of Canins in the Pyrenees on the climb to the finish line at Luz Ardiden. For the first time in three Tours, Maria was on the receiving end of an attack over her favourite terrain, with Longo dishing out the punishment with a new confidence derived from her world championship successes. She beat Canins to the top by a little over a minute to take the yellow jersey.

More changes — and surprises — were still to come. Canins the mountain specialist had been beaten at her own game, so why should she not beat Longo at *her* speciality — the time-trial?

That is exactly what the Italian did, winning the 23.5-km race against the clock at Saint-Nizier. Longo, the race leader, had the advantage of starting last (wearers of the yellow jersey always start last in the time-trials, the second-placed rider immediately in front and so on to the last rider, who starts first) but she could not match the Italian, despite knowing how she was faring from roadside information. She was beaten by 22 seconds, enough to give Canins the yellow jersey.

For the next three days Maria kept her lead, but with one last chance before the flat roads to Paris, Jeannie Longo went for gold on the road between Cluses and Morzine, not far from the Swiss borders.

There was just the one climb of note, the Col de Joux-Plane, which is often used by the men's race as the gateway to the Alpine holiday town. It is a difficult seven-mile climb rising to a height of 5,600 feet. Before its actual summit there is a false piece of downhill, then the final ascent which leads to a very dangerous, twisting plunge through woods to Morzine.

The pair climbed together until near the top Longo put in an acceleration that Canins could not match. She passed over alone, leading by 1 minute 11 seconds, and showed great skill and nerve, descending like a falling stone to finish almost three minutes ahead in Morzine. She had won her first Tour Féminin. In the event she had achieved her victory by using her undoubted skills as an all-round rider. Canins, almost forty, had entered the sport too late to learn the basic riding skills that come more easily to a rider who has grown up in the sport. Longo, at twenty-eight, had now won every major title in the sport.

The older rider, whose strength had carried her through the mountains and the time-trials, was not prepared to take risks on the gravelled descent, and this may have cost her the race. There were only two days left to go, and nothing to spoil Longo's finest hour.

Before the 1988 Tour, Jeannie Longo had spent many hours stamping around her local hills — the Alps! She worked on her weakest points to make sure she could handle Maria Canins when it came to the defence of her title.

As a result of her efforts, the French champion showed such improvement that she won at Morzine and Ste Marie de Campan after crossing three mountains, and finished only 15 seconds behind Canins at the top of the Puy de Dôme, the last challenge of the race.

There was a price to pay — a small one — for in her specialist event, the time-trial, she showed that she had lost some of her speed as a result of her mountain training, being beaten by Monique Knol from Holland in the prologue at Strasbourg. A single second was the margin, and this prevented Longo from leading the race from start to finish.

This was the year, according to the Soviet team manager Mikhail Ioudine, that his team were going to excel. In 1987 they had come to learn. Well, 1988 turned out to be the second lesson, because old hand Kibardina was best finisher in ninth place and there were no Soviet stage victories.

It was a lack-lustre race dominated by Longo, whose professional approach to racing and preparation left the finish a foregone conclusion. The race did nothing to enhance the spectators' interest.

In all, the French riders won nine of the 13 stages, Monique Knol — who later became the Olympic champion in Seoul — won two, and Maria Canins also two. Where were the rest of the 77 riders who finished from the 79 starters?

1985:
1.176 km (Two races linked together of 793 km and 383 km).
1st Race — La Gacilly to St Étienne.
1. Maria Canins (I) 23–32–09; 2. J. Longo (F) at 13–14; 3. Hines (USA at 22–06; 4. C. Odin (F) at 23–01; 5. D. Damiani (F) at 24–25; 6. I. Chiappa (I) at 24–44.
2nd Race — Laguepie to Paris (Champs-Élysées).
1. Maria Canins (I) 17,141 pts. 2. J. Longo (F) 15,810 (at 22 min 11 sec); 3. C. Odi (Fr) 15,052 (34–49); 4. I. Chiappa (I) 14,906 (37–15); 5. R. Bonanomi (I) 14,821 (38–40); 6. C. Broca (F) 14,977 (39–04).
British: 15. Judith Painter, 14,301; 22. Maria Blower, 13,605; 27. Catherine Swinnerton, 13,179; 30. Linda Gornall, 12,898; 56. Pauline Strong, 9,887.
Points: Jeannie Longo.
Mountains: Maria Canins.
Team: Italy.

1986:
996 km.
1. Maria Canins (I) 27–23–37; 2. J. Longo (F) at 15–31; 3. I. Thompson (USA) at 22–09; 4. V. Simmonet (F) at 34–31; 5. E. Hepple (Australia) at 35–25; 6. S. Schumacher (WG) at 38–04.
British: 18. Clare Greenwood at 44–55; 29. Sue Thompson at 56–31; 42. Denise Burton at 1–14–16; 58. Louise Kershaw at 1–36–33; 65. Maxine Johnson at 1–55–02; 74. Katherine Miles at 2–53–44.
Points: Jeannie Longo.
Mountains: Maria Canins.
Team: Italy.

1987:
983 km
1. Jeannie Longo (Fr) 27–33–36; 2. M. Canins (It) at 2–52; 3. U. Enzenauer (WG) at 12–14; 4. T. Poliakova (USSR) at 16–06; 5. R. Bonanomi (It) at 17–37; 6. U. Larsen (Norway) at 20–32.
British: 24. Clare Greenwood at 5–28; 27. Sue Thompson at 49–13; 61. Pauline Strong at 1–31–41; 63. Vicki Thomas at 1–34–0; 69. Melanie Grivell at 1–38–40; 71. Helen Edwards at 1–56–05.
Points: Jeannie Longo.
Mountains: Maria Canins.
Team: France A.
1988:
838 km
1. Jeannie Longo (Fr) 22-41-33; 2. Maria Canins (It) at 1-20; 3. Liz Hepple (Aust) at 13-04; 4. Tea Vikstedt-Nyman (Fin) at 15-30; 5. Imelda Chiappa (Is) at 17-01; 6. Cécile Odin (Fr) at 17-38.
British: 16. Clare Greenwood at 22-67; 36. Sue Gornall at 36-28; 67. Judith Painter at 1-13-56; 76. Theresa Coltman at 1-35-27; 77. Melanie Garvell at 1-43-47.
Points: Jeannie Longo
Mountains: Maria Canins
Team: Italy

Au Revoir, Jeannie?

After her victory in last summer's Tour Féminin, Jeannie Longo became the complete rider; in the heat of the Alps she had added the last required ability — that of climbing — to make herself the most accomplished woman cylcist in the world. But thirst for success makes every achievement ephemeral to a champion, and by the end of last summer Jeannie Longo was thinking only of her failure to win the Olympic title in Seoul.

In Korea she was a pitiful sight, dangling at the back of the field in the road race, knowing that her leg — injured a few weeks before — could not take her to the one title she is now certain never to win. Her hopes of a unique season — winning the world pursuit crown, the Tour Féminin, the team time-trial and the Olympic title had ended at the third fence when she fell while leading her team to almost certain victory in the time-trial in Belgium. She sustained a hair-line leg fracture.

Nevertheless, even if Jeannie had recovered and won the Olympic title in Seoul, would she have retired with the world championships in France this summer? She now has the renewed incentive to aim for gold.

Whether the girl who has dominated French racing for more than a decade will ride the Tour de France again is debatable, as she has nothing further to prove — she has simply been the best.

World Performances
Road Race
1981 — Czechoslovakia — 2nd
1985 — Italy — 1st
1986 — United States — 1st
1987 — Austria — 1st

Track Records
 3km: indoor & outdoor
 5km: indoor
10km: indoor & outdoor
20km: indoor & outdoor
Hour: indoor & outdoor

Pursuit
1982 — England — 3rd
1983 — Switzerland — 3rd
1984 — Spain — 2nd
1985 — Italy — 2nd
1986 — United States — 1st
1987 — Austria — 2nd
1988 — Belgium — 1st

Chapter 10
The Tour 1989

This year the Tour de France has 'only' 3,215 km in 21 racing days. It will be the target of many riders who believe they are in with more than just a chance of winning the world's greatest race.

Despite a return to the 23-day period — after a year's enforced reduction by the international federation FICP (Féderation Internationale du Cyclisme Professional) — the organizers have actually reduced the race in distance, making it 100 miles a day average, the shortest since 1905. It is another brave gamble from the Société, but in the end it is the way the riders race the course that makes for a great Tour. This one has all the ingredients to be just that.

There may be more sinister reasoning too — that following the doping scandals of last year, the organization is hoping that the shorter race will provide less temptation to the riders to use stimulants.

With the expansion in recent years of the racing calendar, and the subsequent demands placed on professional riders, the Tour has become the longest marathon of many, leaving the riders too exhausted to race the complete distance. This new formula might help to provide the answer.

The Tour has continued the reshuffle of its executives which began when Félix Levitan resigned in 1987, partially with the aim of making the race easier to understand.

Gone are two classifications — the team race on points, where the team leaders wore green hats, and the white jersey worn by the best young rider, although the prize for the best young finisher will remain. Like last year, the race will retain its formula of 22 teams of nine riders, which seemed a success as the smaller teams were less able to control the attacks by others.

The distance may be short, but the road will be tough between the Grand Duchy of Luxembourg and the open spaces of the Champs-Élysées in the centre of Paris, with plenty of opportunity for the visitor to watch the race. There will be 11 stages over flattish roads, six in the mountains and four very important time-trials. The most surprising aspect of a new-look Tour is the last stage from the beautiful château at Versailles to the Champs-Élysées. This will be an individual time-trial designed to keep everyone guessing as to the final winner, until the last stage is over.

The last time the race ended as a time-trial was in 1971, also from Versailles, when Eddy Merckx confirmed his victory by winning in Paris, but undoubtedly the finest finish ever came in 1968 when bespectacled Dutchman Jan Janssen 'robbed' Herman Van Springel of final victory during the last time-trial from Melun to Paris. Never having worn the leader's jersey throughout the race, Janssen went home as winner overall by 38 seconds — still the closest result on record — after the unhappy Belgian leader could only end the last-day time-trial second to Janssen.

For only the tenth time in history, the 76th Tour de France begins away from home, and for the first time in one of Europe's smallest countries — Luxembourg. The Duchy, situated in the centre of Western Europe, has always played a role in the race, being remembered best for producing the great climber Charly Gaul, who earned the nickname 'Angel of the Mountains'. Gaul is now fifty-seven, he has grown a beard and put on a bit of weight, but his exploits as 1958 winner will always be remembered with fondness.

Previously the race has passed through Luxembourg during a daily stage across the nation. In 1947 the only stage ended there, won by the Italian Aldo Ronconi. This time, after two years in preparation, the city of Luxembourg and its surrounds are ready to celebrate in style with a Prologue time-trial, a road race and a team time-trial. For the race. It is a familiar start-pattern these days.

Fortunately, the Tour has reverted to its anti-clockwise journey around France, which means that the Pyrenees comes before the Alps, and they in turn end ony three days before the race itself. It will be a difficult race for the hopefuls to 'read', and energy will need to be conserved for the right opportunity to arise. Certainly by the time the field flies from the Belgian borders at Lille to Brittany, the leader will more than likely only be a pretender to the yellow jersey.

The Belgian Ardennes are, as any touring motorist knows, welcoming and beautiful. The villages are on wooded hillsides, and the roads, often long white concrete strips, are pleasing to the eye. A far cry indeed from the inhospitable countryside that greeted the allied armies of the World Wars. From Liège, heartland of the Ardennes, where French instead of Flemish is the spoken ton-

Greg LeMond missed the 1987 Tour after he was accidentally shot by his brother-in-law in a hunting accident. Now the American is back, hoping to repeat his 1986 victory.

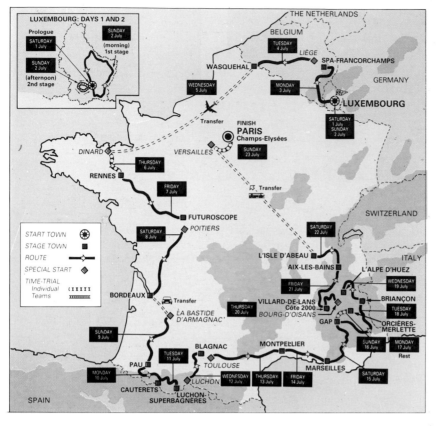

gue, and where Gino Bartali, André Darrigade and Rik Van Looy are listed among the most famous stage winners, the race heads to France.

Sean Yates won in Wasquehal last year, a win he will always remember, but this time the stage will be a road race and not a time-trial, so the sprinters will be to the fore. The transfer carries the race over Normandy to Dinard, a town that the race has passed by for twenty years, but which will now return to the limelight as the riders face a testing and long individual time-trial of 79 km to Rennes. This will be the longest individual test since 1985, and if Pedro Delgado is to defend his title successfully then he will do his best to limit his losses here and hope to make up ground in the mountain finishes.

The result of the time-trial will decide the tactics for the trip down to the Pyrenees, which is over familiar territory. After the longest time-trial comes the longest stage of the race — 259 km to Futuroscope.

Futuroscope — from where the Tour will start in 1990 — is a town and industrial centre representing the shape of things to come. If you are a traditionalist — and I am — you will not like what you see at this new settlement near Poitiers. The Tour has been visiting since 1986, and the mud is gradually clearing in favour of buildings that might find a better home on Mars!

On to Bordeaux, the most visited city (apart from Paris) and then the mountains approach — the holiday is over.

La Bastide d'Armagnac, a first for the small town 80 km south of Bordeaux, opens the eighth stage of 201 km to Pau and the gateway to the Pyrenees.

Facing the riders next morning are four cols and a climb to the finish at Cauterets on the Spanish border, a spa settlement ignored by the Tour for thirty-six years.

The French side of the Pyrenees give little choice of roads, most going to the top and ending there, so the next day the riders face a shorter twisting route of 141 km between Cauterets and Superbagnères, but instead of distance they have to cope with the severe terrain.

The 76th Tour route at a glance

Saturday, 1 July, Prologue Luxembourg, 6.5 km (4 miles).

Sunday, 2 July, stage 1 Luxembourg circuit, 120 km (74.6 miles). Stage 2, team time-trial, 30 km (18.6 miles).

Monday 3 July, stage 3 Luxembourg to Spa-Francorchamps, 189 km (117 miles).

Tuesday, 4 July, stage 4 Liège to Wasquehal, 203 km (126 miles).

Wednesday, 5 July, transfer to Dinard, no racing.

Thursday, 6 July, stage 5 Dinard to Rennes, time-trial, 79 km (49 miles).

Superbagnères is 19 km away from Luchon, a beautiful spa and casino town which is always packed with holidaymakers and, like all the Pyrenean towns, without enough hotel accommodation.

The Tour will stay on the mountain, opening ski chalets for the night to rest the weary legs after the long 18 km climb to 1,805 metres — and the finishing line! Add to this dreadful day the Col du Tourmalet (2,115 metres) col d'Aspin (1,490) and the col de Peyresourde (1,569), and the spectators will have a marvellous day out. The Tour will have begun!

The race then leaves the Pyrenees for Blagnac, a town which is really an extension of Toulouse airport, although I doubt whether the residents would like me saying so.

The threat of torrential rain in this area was realized two years ago when the stage was almost washed out as sewers burst and riders finished literally on the crest of a wave.

On to Montpellier, where the medieval city welcomes the race for the first time in nine years. This stage — the twelfth — crosses the undulations of the Languedoc countryside, missed last year because of the long airlink between the Alps and the Pyrenees.

Following the indentations of the Mediterranean, the race then noses its way towards the Alps by way of Marseilles, France's oldest town, founded by the Greeks in the sixth century BC. It was first discovered by the Tour in 1903, the race commencing the seventy-six to date. Surprisingly the race has passed by the city since 1971, so 1989 could be quite a homecoming, especially on 14 July — Bastille day — to the city that provided France's national anthem. From Marseilles, the survivors face a long ride of 233 km to Gap through the beautiful Dauphiné, and the last of the 'easy' days before the Alps are reached. Orcières-Merlette is a resort at the end of a road to nowhere, high in the Alps. In the summer it is a wonderful escape from reality, but for the Tour riders it will prove for many the road to oblivion.

For the first time, Orcières-Merlette sees the race arriving as an individual time-trial of 42 km, and this will set the trend for the rest of the last week of the race because each rider will have to struggle to the top of the 14-km climb to the village, which rests at 1,817 metres. After the storm comes a temporary calm, as the riders discover the other face of this fine resort, spending a free day there on 17 July. Outside their chalet windows they will be able to see the peaks of the mountains that will assuredly finalize the race in the remaining few days.

Returning down to Gap, the race heads back into the Alps on the last Tuesday, 174 km to Briançon. Two of the most revered climbs in Tour history await them — the Col de Vars (2,210 metres) and the Col de l'Izoard (2,360 metres) — before the finish at the Citadel in Briançon.

Friday, 7 July, stage 6
Rennes to Futuroscope, 259 km (161 miles).

Saturday, 8 July, stage 7
Poitiers to Bordeaux, 258.5 km (161 miles).

Sunday, 9 July, stage 8
La Bastide d'Armagnac to Pau, 201 km (125 miles).

Monday, 10 July, stage 9
Pau to Cauterets, 201.5 km (125 miles).

Tuesday, 11 July, stage 10
Cauterets to Luchon (Superbagnères) 141 km (88 miles).

Wednesday, 12 July, stage 11
Luchon to Blagnac, 162 km (101 miles).

Thursday, 13 July, stage 12
Toulouse to Montpellier, 233 km (145 miles).

Friday, 14 July, stage 13
Montpellier to Marseilles, 168 km (104 miles).

Saturday, 15 July, stage 14
Marseilles to Gap, 233.5 km (145 miles).

Sunday, 16 July, stage 15
Gap to Orcières-Merlette, time-trial, 42 km (26 miles).

Monday, 17 July, rest day, no racing.

Tuesday, 18 July, stage 16
Gap to Briançon, 174 km (108 miles).

Wednesday, 19 July, stage 17
Briançon to l'Alpe d'Huez, 162 km (101 miles).

Thursday, 20 July, stage 18
Bourg d'Oisans to Villard-de Lans (Côte 2000) 90.5 km (56 miles).

Friday, 21 July, stage 19
Villard-de-Lans to Aix-les-Bains, 124 km (77 miles).

Saturday, 22 July, stage 20
Aix-les-Bains to l'Isle
  d'Abeau (Hewlett
  Packard) 110 km (68
  miles),

Sunday, 23 July, stage 21
Versailles to Paris
  (Champs-
  Élysées—Tuileries) time-
  trial, 27 km (17 miles)
Total distance (approx.)
  3,215 km (1,998 miles).
Average per day is 161 km
  (100 miles).

The mountain-storming continues unabated the next day when the giant of them all, the Col du Galibier, is crossed during a cruel day of 162 km between Briançon and l'Alpe d'Huez.

The road to Alpe d'Huez from Bourg d'Oisans has been ridden by thousands of cyclists over the past few years, and as anyone who has tried will testify, to ride the most famous mountain in recent Tour history is a harrowing experience. The great Italian Fausto Coppi was the first to conquer the slope in 1952, and along with that of Louison Bobet, the triple French winner of the Tour, Coppi's memorial can be seen on the side of the climb. There are two plaques, side by side, with each man's sculptured profile.

Recently the climb has become the somewhat personal property of Pedro Delgado, last year's winner, whose memories are of both sadness and joy.

He retired on the climb when lying fifth three years ago on hearing of the death of his mother. In 1987 he won his first yellow jersey there, and the tears flowed again as he dedicated it to his mother. Then, last year, drawn by forces outside sporting ambition, Delgado took the lead again, this time keeping it to the finish.

The race leaves the high Alps with four days left, racing to Côte 2000, a climb on the outskirts of Villard-de-Lans. This had less happy memories for Delgado last year as when the stage was a time-trial, he gave the now infamous 'positive' dope test after winning the stage from Grenoble.

As one leaves Villard and its lush green countryside, the Alps are forgotten while the fields unwind along the road to Aix-les-

The col d'Aubisque in the Pyrenees was the scene for Stephen Roche's first stage win in 1985. This time the mountain is included on Stage 9, during a cruel stage of 201 km from Pau to Cauterets.

The Alps are stunningly beautiful to everyone except perhaps the riders! This is the road to Alpe d'Huez, with Borg d'Oisans in the valley. In 1989 these roads may again prove decisive in the tour.

Bains. With no more hills to worry about, the front runners will concentrate on defending their gains and keeping out of trouble while undoubtedly thinking of the last time-trial to Paris.

If this last stage approaches the excitement of 1968 — when Herman Van Springel lost the stage by 54 seconds — turning his 16 seconds overnight lead into a 38 seconds defeat — then the new Tour finish which has to be seen as an interesting gamble will be seen as another success for the Société du Tour de France!

The principal difficulties at a glance

Sunday, 2 July
Team Time-trial

Thursday, 6 July
Individual Time-trial

Monday, 10 July
Col de Labays, Col d'Ichère, Col de Marie-Blanque, Col d'Aubisque, finishing climb to Cauterets.

Tuesday, 11 July
Col du Tourmalet, Col d'Aspin, Col de Peyresourde, finishing climb to Superbagnères.

Wednesday, 12 July
Col des Ares.

Sunday, 16 July
Finishing climb to Merlette.

Tuesday, 18 July
Col de Vars, Col de l'Izoard, finishing climb to La Citadelle.

Wednesday, 19 July
Col du Lautaret, Col du Galibier, Col de la Croix de Fer, finishing climb to Alpe d'Huez.

Thursday, 20 July
Finishing climb to Côte 2000.

Friday, 21 july
Col de Porte, Col de Cucheron, Col du Granier.

Sunday, 23 July
Individual Time-trial to Paris.

Pedro Delgado led the Tour in 1987 before Roche finally took the lead off him with a day to go. In 1988 he went one better to take the supreme prize.

*Colombia are waiting for the big day when they win for the first time. Fabio Parra (**left**) and Luis Herrera are the front runners of the South American challenge.*

For the record — the top 30 of 1988

1. Pedro Delgado (Spain) 84 hours 27 min 53 sec
2. Steven Rooks (Holland) at 7 min 13 sec behind
3. Fabio Parra (Colombia) at 9−58
4. Steve Bauer (Canada) at 12−15
5. Eric Boyer (France) at 14−4
6. Luis Herrera (Colombia) at 14−36
7. Ronan Pensec (France) at 16−52
8. Alvaro Pino (Spain) at 18−36
9. Peter Winnen (Holland) at 19−12
10. Denis Roux (France) at 20−8
11. Gert-Jan Theunisse (Holland) at 22−46
12. Erik Breukink (Holland) at 23−6
13. Laudelino Cubino (Spain) at 23−46
14. Claude Criquielion (Belgium) at 24−32
15. Andy Hampsten (USA) at 26−0
16. Marino Lajaretta (Spain) at 26−36
17. Pascal Simon (France) at 28−39
18. Eric Caritoux (France) at 29−4
19. Jerome Simon (France) at 30−55
20. Raul Alcala (Mexico) at 31−14
21. Gerhard Zadrobilek (Austria) at 32−9
22. Roberto Visentini (Italy) at 33−23
23. Thierry Claveyrolat (France) at 37−49
24. Janus Kuum (Norway) at 38−53
25. Federico Echave (Spain) at 39−17
26. Jorgen Pedersen (Denmark) at 39−24
27. Jorg Mueller (Switzerland) at 40−53
28. Frédéric Vichot (France) at 42−0
29. Peter Stevenhaagen (Holland) at 45−27
30. Eduardo Chozas (Spain) at 45−45

Competition from the Rest of the World

Jean-François Bernard — France
Born: 2 May 1962
Years professional: 5
From: Luzy.
World ranking at start of season: 46
Tour performances:
  1986 − 16th
  1987 − 3rd
  1988 − Did not finish.

Other major performances:
1985 — Stage win in Tour of Switzerland.
1986 — Tour of the Mediterranean.
Stage win in Tour de France.
2nd Tour of Romandy.
46th World championship, USA.
1987 — Leader Paris−Nice (2nd overall in end).
Stage win in Tour of Italy (16th overall in end).
49th World championship, Austria.

Comment: Jean-François has shot to stardom in France because of his fine riding in the 1986 and 1987 Tours, but since then he has not improved. He has been bothered by injury, and because of this made a late start to 1989. He must again show himself to be a Tour candidate.

Eric Boyer — France

Born: 2 December 1963
Years professional: 5
From: Choisy-le-Roi.
World ranking at start of season: 37
Tour performances:
1986 – 98th
1988 – 5th

Other major performances:
1987 — 6th Tour of the Economic Community.
4th Tour of Lombardy.
1988 — 2nd Midi-Libre.

Comment: Eric's fifth place in the Tour de France last year made him the best Frenchman, yet the papers seemed to ignore him, concentrating on the retirement of more fashionable French riders. This year Boyer must prove he was not just a flash in the pan.

Pedro Delgado — Spain

Born: 15 April 1960
Years professional: 8
From: Segovia.
World ranking at start of season: 9

Tour performances:
1983 — 15th
1984 — Did not finish.
1985 — 6th
1986 — Did not finish.
1987 — 2nd
1988 — 1st

Other major performances:
1984 — 4th Tour of Spain.
1985 — Tour of Spain.
Stage win Tour de France.
25th World championship, Italy.
1986 — 6th Tour of Switzerland.
Stage win Tour de France.
51st World championship, USA.
1987 — 4th Tour of Spain.

Comment: Delgado has become a man for the Tour de France. He retired in the Alps on hearing the news of the death of his mother when lying fifth in 1986. Since then the Alps are very special to him, and he has twice since taken the Tour lead there. He will only win the Tour again, however, if the route is hilly enough.

Luis Herrera — Colombia

Born: 4 May 1961
Years professional: 5
From: Fusagasuga.
World ranking at start of season: 26

Other major performances:
1984 — Stage win Tour de France (first Colombian to win).
Tour of Colombia.
Classico RCN.
1985 — Tour of Colombia.
Two stage wins in Tour de France.
King of the Mountains, Tour de France.
1986 — Classico RCN.
Tour of Colombia.
1987 — Tour of Spain (first Colombian winner).
King of the Mountains, Tour de France.
1988 — Dauphiné-Libéré.

Comment: Herrera is a great climber and has improved his ability to time-trial, so this year he could challenge for overall victory in the Tour de France.

Fabio Parra — Colombia

Born: 22 November 1959
Years professional: 5
From: Sogamoso.
World ranking at start of season: 29

Tour Performances:
1985 — 8th
1986 — Did not finish.
1987 — 6th
1988 — 3rd

Other major performances:
1985 — Champion of Colombia.
Stage win in Tour de France.
1986 — 8th Tour of Spain.
1987 — Classico RCN.
3rd Tour of Switzerland.
1988 — 5th Tour of Spain.
Stage win in Tour de France.

Comment: Fabio is one of a terrific duo from South America, and he seems to be the one improving all the time. The duel will continue between Fabio and Luis Herrera, to see who becomes the first Colombian to win the Tour.

On the facing page is a selection of riders likely to contest this year's race. Selections are often made very late, and, even then they are subject to last-minute changes due to injury or sickness. Underneath each rider's name is given his past Tour performances. A nought given after the year indicates that the rider did not finish. (Where two figures are given for a rider's age it indicates that he has a birthday during the Tour.)

The Men Who Have Done It Before — and Hope to Do it Again.

Henri Abadie (France) age 26.
1988/44.

Rafaël Acevedo (Colombia) age 32.
1984/12; 1985/43; 1986/0; 1987/18.

Alfred Achermann (Switzerland) age 30.
1987/86; 1988/125.

Enrique Aja (Spain) age 29.
1983/75; 1984/51; 1985/62; 1986/60; 1987/58; 1988/64.

Raul Alcala (Mexico) age 25.
1986/114; 1987/9 (winner of white jersey); 1988/20.

Stefano Allochio (Italy) age 27.
1986/0; 1987/129.

Phil Anderson (Australia) age 31.
1981/10; 1982/5; 1983/9; 1984/10; 1985/5; 1986/39; 1987/27.

Francisco Antequera (Spain) age 24.
1987/117; 1988/121.

Dominique Arnaud (France) age 33.
1981/24; 1982/36; 1983/26; 1984/54; 1985/22; 1986/76; 1987/0; 1988/48.

Angel Arroyo (Spain) age 32.
1983/2; 1984/6; 1985/0; 1987/0; 1988/0.

Jean-Claude Bagot (France) age 31.
1984/0; 1985/65; 1986/19; 1987/33; 1988/39.

Steve Bauer (Canada) age 30.
1985/10; 1986/23; 1987/74; 1988/4.

Vincente Belda (Spain) age 34.
1980/20; 1981/38; 1988/75.

Charly Berard (France) age 33.
1981/27; 1982/16; 1983/56; 1984/49; 1986/44; 1987/59; 1988/40.

Marco Bergamo (Italy) age 25.
1988/109.

Jean-François Bernard (France) age 27.
1986/16; 1987/3; 1988/0.

Jean-René Bernaudeau (France) age 32/33.
1978/0; 1979/5; 1980/0; 1981/6; 1982/13; 1983/6; 1984/0; 1985/0; 1986/26; 1987/17.

Michel Bibollet (France) age 26.
1985/133; 1988/88.

Andy Bishop (USA) age 28.
1988/135.

Jesus Blanco (Spain) age 27.
1986/25; 1987/0; 1988/35.

Argemiro Bohorquez (Colombia) age 29.
1986/0; 1987/69.

Guido Bontempi (Italy) age 29.
1982/0; 1985/112; 1986/92; 1987/119; 1988/106.

Philippe Bouvatier (France) age 25.
1986/0; 1987/66; 1988/32.

Eric Boyer (France) age 25.
1986/98; 1988/5.

Beat Breu (Switzerland) age 33.
1982/6; 1983/22; 1984/43; 1985/23; 1986/74; 1987/26.

Erik Breukink (Holland) age 25.
1987/21; 1988/12.

Frédéric Brun (France) age 31.
1980/75; 1982/66; 1983/78; 1984/89; 1985/134; 1986/107; 1987/92; 1988/81.

Gianni Bugno (Italy) age 25.
1988/62.

Samuel Cabrera (Colombia) age 28.
1983/57; 1984/32; 1986/11; 1987/0; 1988/31.

Julio-Caesar Cadena (Colombia) age 25.
1987/46; 1988/42.

Angel Camarillo (Spain) age 30.
1986/0; 1988/116.

Eric Caritoux (France) age 28.
1983/24; 1984/24; 1985/34; 1986/20; 1987/23; 1988/18.

Chris Carmichael (USA) age 28.
1986/0.

Jean-Carlos Castillo (Colombia) age 24.
1987/36.

Philippe Casado (France) age 25.
1988/129.

André Chappuis (France) age 33.
1982/114; 1983/0; 1984/67; 1986/118; 1987/123.

Eduardo Chozas (Spain) age 28/29.
1985/9; 1986/14; 1987/25; 1988/30.

Jean-Claude Colotti (France) age 28.
1987/0; 1988/55.

Bruno Cornillet (France) age 26.
1986/0; 1987/37; 1988/0.

Thierry Claveyrolat (France) age 30.
 1985/29; 1986/17; 1987/0; 1988/23.
Régis Clere (France) age 32.
 1981/51; 1982/45; 1983/0; 1984/0; 1987/72;
 1988/94.
Edgar Corredor (Colombia) age 29.
 1983/16; 1984/0; 1985/0; 1986/0; 1988/41.
Israel Corredor (Colombia) age 29.
 1984/78; 1986/106; 1988/49.
Claude Criquielion (Belgium) age 32.
 1979/9; 1980/13; 1981/9; 1982/0; 1984/9;
 1985/18; 1986/5; 1987/11; 1988/14.
Laudelino Cubino (Spain) age 26.
 1987/0; 1988/13.
Nathan Dahlberg (New Zealand) age 24.
 1988/144.
Acacio Da Silva (Portugal) age 28;
1986/82; 1987/64. 1988/92.
Jacques Decrion (France) age 27.
 1988/72.
Roque De La Cruz (Spain) age 24.
 1987/52; 1988/104.
Pedro Delgado (Spain) age 29.
 1983/15; 1984/0; 1985/6; 1986/0; 1987/2;
 1988/1.
Dirk De Mol (Belgium) age 29.
 1985/0; 1988/149.
Michel Dernies (Belgium) age 28.
 1985/96; 1986/113; 1987/115.
Theo De Rooy (Holland) age 32.
1981/39; 1982/19; 1983/29; 1984/59; 1985/
 80; 1987/91; 1988/0.
Hendrik De Vos (Belgium) age 33.
1979/31; 1980/63; 1981/57; 1982/88; 1983/
 63; 1984/88; 1985/58; 1986/43; 1987/0.
Etienne De Wilde (Belgium) age 31.
 1982/0; 1983/0; 1984/0; 1988/103.
Alphonse De Wolfe(Belgium) age 33.
 1981/11; 1982/31; 1984/74; 1985/0; 1988/
 102.
Dirk De Wolf (Belgium) age 28.
 1986/65; 1988/80.
Rudy Dhaenens (Belgium) age 28.
 1983/0; 1984/0; 1985/101; 1986/122; 1987/
 0; 1988/87.
Pedro Diaz-Zabala (Spain) age 26/27.
 1988/118.
Raimund Dietzen (West Germany) age 30.
 1982/0; 1984/64; 1986/0; 1987/90; 1988/83.
Manuel-Jorge Domingues (Spain) age 26.
 1987/118; 1988/128.
Gilbert Duclos-Lassalle (France) age 34.
 1979/46; 1980/0; 1981/28; 1982/60; 1983/
 59; 1985/61; 1986/0; 1987/80 (red jersey
 winner); 1988/36.

Maarten Ducrot (Holland) age 30.
 1985/84; 1986/81; 1987/0.
Martin Earley (Ireland) age 27.
 1985/60; 1986/46; 1987/65; 1988/0.
Federico Echave (Spain) age 28/29.
 1984/39; 1986/38; 1987/12; 1988/25.
Malcolm Elliott (England) age 28.
 1987/94; 1988/90.
Patrice Esnault (France) age 28.
 1986/0; 1987/0; 1988/78.

Laurent Fignon (France) age 28.
 1983/1; 1984/1; 1986/0; 1987/7; 1988/0.
Robert Forest (France) age 27.
 1985/16; 1986/35; 1987/38.
Herman Frison (Belgium) age 28.
 1987/122.
Anselmo Fuerte (Spain) age 27.
 1985/109; 1986/31; 1987/8; 1988/0.
Dominique Gaigne (France) age 27/28.
 1983/65; 1984/121; 1985/116; 1986/85.
Dominique Garde (France) age 30.
 1982/64; 1983/40; 1984/33; 1985/35; 1986/
 45; 1987/54; 1988/93.
Frédéric Garnier (France) age 25.
 1988/108.
Inaki Gaston (Spain) age 26.
 1985/38; 1986/75; 1987/0; 1988/112.
Jean-Louis Gauthier (France) age 33.
 1978/69; 1979/50; 1980/50; 1981/58; 1982/
 104; 1983/76; 1984/97; 1985/69; 1986/0;
 1987/134.
Bernard Gavillet (Switzerland) age 29.
 1983/34; 1984/20; 1986/28; 1987/57.

Martial Gayant (France) age 28.
1985/0; 1987/34; 1988/71.
Massimo Ghirotto (Italy) age 28.
1987/109; 1988/85.
Gilbert Glaus (Switzerland) age 33.
1982/105; 1983/85; 1984/124; 1986/0;
1987/0.
Jan Goessens (Belgium) age 26.
1987/131.
Rolf Golz (West Germany) age 26.
1987/49; 1988/91.
Marc Gomez (France) age 34.
1982/71; 1983/0; 1985/99; 1986/123; 1987/
79.
Arsensio Gonzalez (Spain) age 29.
1988/97.
Julian Gorospe (Spain) age 29.
1983/0; 1984/52; 1986/79; 1987/83; 1988/
60.
Alfonso Guttierrez (Spain) age 27.
1986/0; 1987/0; 1988/0.
Jos Haex (Belgium) age 29.
1986/78; 1987/71; 1988/56.
Paul Haghedooren (Belgium) age 29.
1983/49; 1984/0; 1985/33; 1986/67.
Andrew Hampsten (USA) age 27.
1986/4; 1987/16; 1988/15.
Jacques Hanegraaf (Holland) age 28.
1984/101; 1988/119.
Mathieu Hermans (Holland) age 26.
1986/0; 1987/135; 1988/147.
Carlos Hernandez (Spain) age 30.
1983/55; 1984/53; 1985/76; 1986/53; 1987/
128; 1988/0.
Omar Hernandez (Colombia) age 29.
1986/0; 1987/24; 1988/0.
Jesus Hernandez-Ubeda (Spain) age 29
1983/54; 1984/71; 1985/85; 1986/117;
1987/108.
Luis Herrera (Colombia) age 27.
1984/27; 1985/7; 1986/22; 1987/5; 1988/6.
Jean-Pierre Heynderickx (Belgium) age 23.
1988/148.
Peter Hilse (West Germany) age 27.
1987/106.
Frank Hoste (Belgium) age 33.
1980/0; 1981/95; 1982/0; 1984/100; 1986/
116; 1987/0; 1988/124.
Heinz Imboden (Switzerland) age 27.
1987/0.
Miguel Indurain (Spain) age 24/25.
1985/0; 1986/0; 1987/97; 1988/47.
Gert Jakobs (Holland) age 25.
1987/0; 1988/145.
Carlos Jaramillo (Colombia) age 28.
1985/73; 1986/55; 1987/0.

Patrocinio Jiminez (Colombia) age 36.
1983/17; 1984/15; 1986/21; 1988/51.
Milan Jurco (Czechoslovakia) age 31.
1987/0; 1988/139.
Andreas Kappes (West Germany) age 23.
1988/110.
Sean Kelly (Ireland) age 33.
1978/34; 1979/38; 1980/29; 1981/48; 1982/
15; 1983/7; 1984/5; 1985/4; 1987/0; 1988/
46.
Ron Kiefel (USA) age 29.
1986/96; 1987/82; 1988/69.
Paul Kimmage (Ireland) age 27.
1986/131; 1987/0.
Gerrie Knetemann (Holland) age 38.
1974/38; 1975/63; 1976/0; 1977/31; 1978/
43; 1979/30; 1980/38; 1981/55; 1982/47;
1984/103; 1986/84; 1987/89; 1988/0.
Janus Kuum (Norway) age 24.
1988/24.
José Laguia (Spain) age 29.
1983/0; 1984/41; 1985/0; 1986/121; 1987/
43.
Marino Lajarreta (Spain) age 32.
1981/35; 1982/37; 1986/18; 1987/10; 1988/
16.
Johan Lammerts (Holland) age 28.
1983/72; 1985/75; 1988/130.
Dag-Otto Lauritzen (Norway) age 29.
1986/34; 1987/59; 1988/34.
Christophe Lavainne (France) age 25.
1985/0; 1986/88; 1987/40; 1988/67.
Bruno Leali (Italy) age 31.
1979/77; 1982/76; 1984/76; 1985/0; 1986/
73; 1988/77.
Jean-Claude Leclercq (France) age 26/27.
1986/56; 1987/50; 1988/58.
Roland Leclerc (France) age 26.
1987/107; 1988/70.
Philippe Leleu (France) age 31.
1983/41; 1984/0; 1986/97; 1988/65.
François Lemarchand (France) age 28.
1985/81; 1986/68; 1987/75.
Greg LeMond (USA) age 28.
1984/3; 1985/2; 1986/1.
Antonio Leon (Colombia) age 26.
1986/86; 1987/44; 1988/73.
Jef Lieckens (Belgium) age 30.
1985/130; 1986/129; 1987/132.
Sören Lilholt (Denmark) age 23.
1988/99.
Henk Lubberding (Holland) age 35.
1977/26; 1978/8; 1979/18; 1980/10; 1981/
54; 1982/46; 1983/10; 1984/40; 1985/82;
1986/0; 1987/95; 1988/0.

Javier Lukin (Spain) age 25.
1987/0; 1988/82.

Frans Maassen (Holland) age 24.
1988/126.

Marc Madiot (France) age 30.
1982/30; 1983/8; 1984/35; 1985/26; 1987/47; 1988/66.

Yvon Madiot (France) age 27.
1984/46; 1985/72; 1986/10; 1987/73; 1988/0.

Erich Maechler (Switzerland) age 28.
1983/84; 1984/84; 1985/114; 1986/49; 1987/85; 1988/136.

Walter Magnago (Italy) age 28.
1986/0; 1988/141.

Thierry Marie (France) age 26.
1985/67; 1986/108; 1987/87; 1988/98.

René Martens (Belgium) age 32.
1978/26; 1979/25; 1980/30; 1981/83; 1982/24; 1983/0; 1984/68; 1988/131.

Juan Martinez-Olivier (Spain) age 27.
1988/134.

Gilles Mas (France) age 28.
1984/29; 1985/37; 1986/47; 1987/32; 1988/0.

Robert Millar (Scotland) age 30.
1983/14; 1984/4; 1985/11; 1986/0; 1987/19; 1988/0.

Nestor Mora (Colombia) age 25.
1985/118; 1986/83; 1987/63.

Stefaan Morjean (Belgium) age 29.
1985/0; 1986/0; 1987/93; 1988/101.

Charly Mottet (France) age 26.
1985/36; 1986/16; 1987/4; 1988/0.

Jorg Mueller (Switzerland) age 28.
1986/99; 1987/99; 1988/27.

Joaquim Mujika (Spain) age 26.
1985/45; 1986/30; 1987/41; 1988/63.

Pedro Munoz (Spain) age 30.
1984/8; 1985/0; 1986/0; 1987/22; 1988/0.

Javier Murguialday (Spain) age 27.
1987/0; 1988/114.

Jose-Louis Navarro (Spain) age 26.
1987/113.

Jan Nevens (Belgium) age 30.
1981/0; 1986/51; 1987/0; 1988/61.

Erwin Nijboer (Holland) age 25.
1986/0; 1987/0; 1988/0.

Jelle Nijdam (Holland) age 25.
1985/115; 1986/0; 1987/124; 1988/122.

Guy Nulens (Holland) age 31.
1980/0; 1981/52; 1982/22; 1983/0; 1984/24; 1985/24; 1986/54; 1987/61; 1988/38.

Fabio Parra (Colombia) age 29.
1985/8; 1986/0; 1987/6; 1988/3.

Rudy Patry (Belgium) age 27.
1985/111; 1987/116.

Jorgen Pedersen (Denmark) age 29.
1985/50; 1986/77; 1987/68; 1988/26.

Ludo Peeters (Belgium) age 35.
1979/3; 1980/8; 1981/59; 1982/34; 1984/57; 1985/48; 1986/69; 1987/96; 1988/89.

Alan Peiper (Australia) age 29.
1984/95; 1985/86; 1987/0.

Joël Pelier (France) age 27.
1985/78; 1986/0; 1988/120.

Ronan Pensec (France) age 25/26.
1986/6; 1988/7.

Davis Phinney (USA) age 29/30.
1986/0; 1987/0; 1988/105.

Jeff Pierce (USA) age 28.
1986/80; 1987/88; 1988/0.

Alvaro Pino (Spain) age 32.
1985/19; 1986/8; 1988/8.

Eddy Planckaert (Belgium) age 30.
1981/0; 1982/0; 1984/0; 1986/0; 1988/115.

Twan Poels(Holland) age 25.
1986/64; 1988/127.

Pascal Poisson (France) age 30.
1982/50; 1983/0; 1984/80; 1985/42; 1986/67.

Alessandro Pozzi (Italy) age 34.
1979/32; 1986/91; 1987/81; 1988/79.

Celestino Prieto (Spain) age 28.
1983/46; 1984/34; 1985/17; 1986/0; 1987/100; 1988/117.

Martin Ramirez (Colombia) age 28.
1984/0; 1986/42; 1987/13; 1988/0.

Jean-François Rault (France) age 31.
1982/74; 1984/82; 1987/77.

Dante Rezze (France) age 26.
1988/100.

Vicente Ridaura (Spain) age 25.
1986/87; 1988/107.

Stephen Roche (Ireland) age 29.
1983/13; 1984/25; 1985/3; 1986/48; 1987/1.

Francisco Rodriguez (Colombia) age 29.
1984/45; 1985/0; 1986/0; 1987/0.

Jesus Rodriguez (Spain) age 29.
1986/40; 1987/78.

Bob Roll (USA) age 28/29.
1986/63; 1987/0.

Toni Rominger (Switzerland) age 28.
1988/68.

Steven Rooks (Holland) age 28.
1983/0; 1985/25; 1986/9; 1987/0; 1988/2.

Luc Roosen (Belgium) age 24.
1986/103; 1987/104.

Denis Roux (France) age 27.
1985/56; 1987/20; 1988/10.

Pello Ruiz-Cabestany (Spain) age 27.
1985/54; 1986/36; 1987/0.
Nikki Ruttimann (Switzerland) age 28.
1984/11; 1985/13; 1986/7; 1987/0; 1988/43.
Mariano Sanchez (Spain) age 30.
1988/57.
José Sanchis (Spain) age 26.
1985/128; 1987/35; 1988/111.
Gilles Sanders (France) age 24.
1987/28; 1988/0.
Eddy Schepers (Belgium) age 33.
1979/15; 1980/26; 1981/16; 1985/14; 1986/
37; 1987/30; 1988/0.
Marc Sergeant (Belgium) age 29.
1984/48; 1985/59; 1986/0; 1987/0; 1988/33.
Jerome Simon (France) age 28.
1984/36; 1985/24; 1987/42; 1988/19.
Pascal Simon (France) age 32.
1980/28; 1982/20; 1983/0; 1984/7; 1985/20;
1986/13; 1987/53; 1988/17.
Regis Simon (France) age 31.
1984/111; 1985/100; 1986/93; 1988/123.
Gerrit Solleveld (Holland) age 28.
1985/110; 1986/101; 1987/127; 1988/132.
Brian Sorensen (Denmark) age 28.
1987/110.
*Peter Stevenhaagen*1987/ (Holland) age 24.
1986/29; 1987/45; 1988/29.
Marco Tabai (Italy) age 27.
1988/146.
John Talen (Holland) age 24.
1988/150.
Gert-Jan Theunisse (Holland) age 26.
1987/48; 1988/11.
Didi Thurau (West Germany) age 34.
1977/5; 1979/10; 1980/0; 1982/0; 1985/0;
1987/0.
Adrian Timmis (England) age 25.
1987/70.
Juan Uzaga (Spain) age 26.
1988/53.
Guido Van Calster (Belgium) age 33.
1979/58; 1980/39; 1981/0; 1986/72; 1987/
31; 1988/0.
Jean-Philippe Vandenbrande (Belgium) age 33.
1982/54; 1984/42; 1985/40; 1986/58; 1987/
76; 1988/37.
Eric Vanderaerden (Belgium) age 27.
1983/0; 1984/90; 1985/87; 1986/125; 1988/
0.
Adrie Van Der Poel (Holland) age 30.
1982/102; 1983/37; 1984/0; 1985/51; 1986/
110; 1987/105; 1988/84.

Wim Van Eynde (Belgium) age 28/29.
1985/93; 1986/102; 1987/126.
Eric Van Lancker (Belgium) age 28.
1986/89; 1987/56; 1988/74.
Marc Van Orsouw (Holland) age 25.
1986/0; 1988/76.
Ennio Vanotti (Italy) age 33.
1986/66; 1987/0; 1988/86.
Jean-Paul Van Poppel (Holland) age 26.
1987/130; 1988/138.
Rik Van Slijke (Belgium) age 26.
1988/137.
Teun Van Vliet (Holland) age 29.
1985/0; 1987/84; 1988/0.
Jens Veggerby (Denmark) age 26.
1988/113.
Gerard Veldscholten (Holland) age 29.
1982/32; 1983/27; 1984/16; 1985/28; 1986/
61; 1988/45.
Nico Verhoeven (Holland) age 27.
1987/0; 1988/143.
Michel Vermotte (France) age 26.
1987/0; 1988/133.
Frédéric Vichot (France) age 30.
1984/23; 1985/31; 1986/100; 1988/28.
Roberto Visentini (Italy) age 32.
1984/0; 1985/49; 1988/22.
Dirk Wayenberg (Belgium) age 33.
1988/151.
Johnny Weltz (Denmark) age 27.
1988/54.
Jan Wijnants (Belgium) age 30.
1982/0; 1983/68; 1985/52; 1986/105; 1987/
121; 1988/96.
Pablo Wilches (Colombia) age 33/34.
1984/0; 1985/0; 1987/0.
Michael Wilson (Australia) age 28.
1988/50.
Peter Winnen (Holland) age 31.
1981/5; 1982/4; 1983/3; 1984/26; 1985/15;
1986/0; 1988/9.
Guido Winterberg (Switzerland) age 26.
1986/127; 1987/112; 1988/0.
Sean Yates (England) age 29.
1984/91; 1985/122; 1986/112; 1987/0;
1988/59.
Gerhard Zadrobilek (Austria) age 28.
1987/14; 1988/21.
Stefano Zanatta (Italy) age 25.
1988/142.
Urs Zimmerman (Switzerland) age 29.
1984/58; 1986/3; 1987/0; 1988/0.

Appendix
The Tour Through The Years

Over the years the final real distances have varied from the published figures. I have decided to amend this table to agree with official information received from the Société du Tour de France.

Date	Dist.	Stages	Starters	Finishers	Av. Speed	Winner
1903	2,428 (km)	6	60	21	25.28 kph	M. Garin
1904	2,388	6	88	23	24.29	H. Cornet
1905	2,975	11	60	24	27.28	L. Trousselier
1906	4,637	13	82	14	24.46	R. Pottier
1907	4,488	14	93	33	28.47	L. Petit-Breton
1908	4,488	14	114	36	28.74	L. Petit-Breton
1909	4,497	14	150	55	28.66	F. Faber (Lux)
1910	4,700	15	110	41	29.68	O. Lapize
1911	5,544	15	84	28	27.32	G. Garrigou
1912	5,229	15	131	41	27.89	O. Defraye (B)
1913	5,387	15	140	25	27.62	P. Thijs (B)
1914	5,414	15	146	54	27.03	P. Thijs (B)
1919	5,560	15	69	10	24.95	F. Lambot (B)
1920	5,503	15	113	22	24.13	P. Thijs (B)
1921	5,484	15	123	38	24.72	L. Scieur (B)
1922	5,375	15	121	38	24.20	F. Lambot (B)
1923	5,386	15	139	48	24.43	H. Pélissier
1924	5,427	15	157	60	23.96	O. Bottecchia (I)
1925	5,430	18	130	49	24.77	O. Bottecchia (I)
1926	5,795	17	126	41	24.06	L. Buysse (B)
1927	5,321	24	142	39	26.84	N. Frantz (Lux)
1928	5,377	22	162	41	27.83	N. Frantz (Lux)
1929	5,286	22	155	60	28.32	M. Dewaele (B)
1930	4,818	21	100	59	27.98	A. Leducq
1931	5,095	24	81	35	28.76	A. Magne
1932	4,502	21	80	57	29.21	A. Leducq
1933	4,395	23	80	40	29.70	G. Speicher
1934	4,363	23	60	39	29.46	A. Magne
1935	4,302	27	93	46	30.56	R. Maes (B)
1936	4,442	27	90	43	31.07	S. Maes (B)
1937	4,415	31	98	46	31.74	R. Lapebie
1938	4,694	25	96	55	31.56	G. Bartali (I)
1939	4,224	28	79	49	31.99	S. Maes (B)
1947	4,640	21	100	53	31.50	J. Robic
1948	4,922	21	120	44	33.40	G. Bartali (I)
1949	4,813	21	120	55	32.12	F. Coppi (I)
1950	4,776	22	116	51	32.78	F. Kubler (Switz)
1951	4,474	24	123	66	31.43	H. Koblet (Switz)
1952	4,807	23	122	78	31.60	F. Coppi (I)
1953	4,485	22	119	76	34.60	L. Bobet
1954	4,495	23	110	69	34.43	L. Bobet
1955	4,855	23	130	69	34.63	L. Bobet

1956	4,528	23	120	88	36.51	R. Walkowiak
1957	4,555	24	120	56	34.51	J. Anquetil
1958	4,319	24	120	78	36.90	C. Gaul (Lux)
1959	4,363	22	120	65	35.24	F. Bahamontes (Sp)
1960	4,272	22	128	81	37.21	G. Nencini (I)
1961	4,394	22	132	72	36.28	J. Anquctil
1962	4,272	24	149	94	37.31	J. Anquetil
1963	4,140	23	130	76	36.46	J. Anquetil
1964	4,505	25	132	81	35.42	J. Anquetil
1965	4,176	24	130	96	36.09	F. Gimondi (I)
1966	4,329	25	130	82	36.60	L. Aimar
1967	4,780	25	130	88	34.75	R. Pingeon
1968	4,662	26	110	63	34.89	J. Janssen (Hl)
1969	4,102	26	129	86	35.30	E. Merckx (B)
1970	4,366	29	150	100	36.49	E. Merckx (B)
1971	3,690	25	129	94	36.92	E. Merckx (B)
1972	3,847	25	132	88	35.37	E. Merckx (B)
1973	4,140	27	132	87	33.92	L. Ocana (Sp)
1974	4,098	27	130	105	35.24	E. Merckx (B)
1975	4,000	25	140	86	34.99	B. Thevenet
1976	4,018	27	130	87	34.82	L. Van Impe (B)
1977	4,093	28	100	53	35.58	B. Thevenet
1978	3,903	24	110	78	34.62	B. Hinault
1979	3,721	25	150	89	36.28	B. Hinault
1980	3,949	25	130	85	35.53	J. Zoetemelk (Hl)
1981	3,766	25	150	121	37.84	B. Hinault
1982	3,523	22	169	125	37.46	B. Hinault
1983	3,757	23	140	88	35.74	L. Fignon
1984	4.021	24	170	124	34.91	L. Fignon
1985	4,107	24	180	144	36.21	B. Hinault
1986	4,093	23	210	132	36.912	G. LeMond (USA)
1987	4,231	25	207	135	37.29	S. Roche (Ire)
1988	3,286	22	198	151	39.142	P. Delgado (Sp)

Country abbreviations: Unless shown, the winners are from France. Lux—Luxembourg; B—Belgium; Ire—Ireland; I—Italy; Switz—Switzerland; Sp—Spain; Hl—Holland; USA—United States of America.

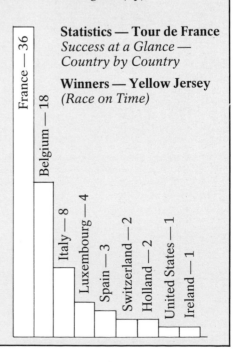

Statistics — Tour de France
*Success at a Glance —
Country by Country*

Winners — Yellow Jersey
(Race on Time)

France — 36
Belgium — 18
Italy — 8
Luxembourg — 4
Spain — 3
Switzerland — 2
Holland — 2
United States — 1
Ireland — 1

Glossary

French is the official language of the Union Cycliste Internationale, the sport's governing body, so many of the terms used in cycling are from the French. In the Tour de France, because of the success of English-speaking riders and those from Scandinavia (where English is a second language) efforts are now being made by the organizers to use the English language as well. Here is a list of French words most commonly used with their approximate significance in English.

Abandon — To give up during the race.
Abri — To take shelter, usually behind a following car!
Accidenté — Used to describe an undulating route, or be injured.
Adjoint — Assistant referee.
Aide entre coureurs — Help between riders.
Amende — A fine for breaking the rules.
Appel — Appeal (against a penalty)
Arrière (roue) — rear (usually a new rear wheel wanted)
Avant — Up front.
Avertissement — Warning.

Balai (voiture) — Last vehicle in race (literally, broom wagon). See also *Voiture balai.*
Bidon — Drinking bottle.
Blesser — Wound or injury.
Bonification — Time bonus
Boyau — Racing tyre.
Braquet — Gear ratio.

Classement — Classification.
Col — Mountain pass.
Commissaire — Referee.
Contre la montre — Time trial.
Coureur — Rider.
Crevaison — Puncture.

Dérailleur — Rear gear mechanism.
Directeur sportif — Team manager
Dossard — Number (on rider).

Écart — Time gap between riders.
Équipe — Team
Équipier — Team-mate.
Étape — Stage (of the race).

Grimpeur — Climbing specialist.
Groupe sportif — Team sponsored by a company
Guidon — Handlebar.

Hors de course — Disqualified.

Maillot — Jersey.
Musette — Food bag carried by riders.

Parcours — Route of race.
Passage à niveau — Level crossing.
Peloton — main field or bunch of riders.

Ravitaillement — Feeding (station).
Roue — Wheel.

Tête (en) — Up front, ahead, in the lead.

Vainqueur — Winner.
Vélo — Bicycle.
Virage — Hairpin bend.
Vitesse — Speed.
Voiture balai — See *Balai voiture*.

Other Information

For those of you in France during the race period all the newspapers cover the event in detail, but the best coverage, naturally, is given by the sponsoring *l'Équipe* and *Le Parisien*. The Tour is on television every afternoon, usually filmed live for the last fifty kilometres. All stages are timed to finish around 5 p.m.

In Britain, *Cycling Weekly* (published every Thursday) gives full detailed coverage of each stage. *Winning Magazine*, which is published monthly with a weekly supplement in July, also covers the race in blow-by-blow detail. For the best daily coverage of the Tour, the newspaper to read is *The Daily Telegraph*.

For further information on cycle racing and touring in Britain and abroad contact:

British Cycling Federation,
36 Rockingham Road, Kettering, Northants, NN16 8HG.
Tel: (0536) 412211

Cyclists' Touring Club,
Cotterell House,
69 Meadrow,
Godalming,
Surrey GU7 3HS.
Tel: (048 68) 7217

The Road Time Trials Council,
Dallacre,
Mill Road
Yarwell,
Peterborough.
PE8 6PS.

TOUR DE FRANCE 1989

LUXEMBOURG: DAYS 1 AND 2

Prologue
SATURDAY 1 July
SUNDAY 2 July (morning) 1st stage
SUNDAY 2 July (afternoon) 2nd stage

THE NETHERLANDS
BELGIUM
TUESDAY 4 July
LIÈGE
WASQUEHAL
SPA-FRANCORCHAMPS
GERMANY
WEDNESDAY 5 July
MONDAY 3 July
STAR **LUXEMBOURG**
SATURDAY 1 July – SUNDAY 2 July

Transfer
FINISH **PARIS** Champs-Elysées
VERSAILLES
SUNDAY 23 July

DINARD
THURSDAY 6 July
RENNES
Transfer
FRIDAY 7 July
SWITZERLAND
FUTUROSCOPE
POITIERS
SATURDAY 8 July
SATURDAY 22 July
L'ISLE D'ABEAU
ITALY
AIX-LES-BAINS
L'ALPE D'HUEZ
FRIDAY 21 July
WEDNESDAY 19 July
VILLARD-DE-LANS Côte 2000
THURSDAY 20 July
BOURG-D'OISANS
BRIANÇON
TUESDAY 18 July

BORDEAUX
Transfer
LA BASTIDE D'ARMAGNAC
GAP
ORCIÈRES-MERLETTE
SUNDAY 9 July
BLAGNAC
MONTPELLIER
SUNDAY 16 July
MONDAY 17 July Rest
TUESDAY 11 July
TOULOUSE
PAU
MARSEILLES
SATURDAY 15 July
MONDAY 10 July
LUCHON
WEDNESDAY 12 July
THURSDAY 13 July
FRIDAY 14 July
CAUTERETS
LUCHON-SUPERBAGNÈRES
SPAIN

Legend:
START TOWN ✸
STAGE TOWN ■
ROUTE ►
SPECIAL START ◆
TIME-TRIAL Individual / Teams

Day 1: Saturday 1 July
Prologue time-trial Luxembourg 6.5 km (4.0 miles)
Stage winner_____

Day 2: Sunday 2 July
Stage 1 Luxembourg to Luxembourg 120 km (74.6 miles)
Stage winner_____
Stage 2 Luxembourg team time-trial 30 km (18.6 miles)
Winning team_____
Overall leader (yellow jersey)_____
Points leader (green jersey)_____
King of the Mountains (polka-dot jersey)_____

Day 3: Monday 3 July
Stage 3 Luxembourg to Spa-Francorchamps 189 km (117 miles)
Stage winner_____
Overall leader_____
Points leader_____
King of the Mountains_____

Day 4: Tuesday 4 July
Stage 4 Liège to Wasquehal 203 km (126 miles)
Stage winner_____
Overall leader_____
Points leader_____
King of the Mountains_____

Day 5: Wednesday 5 July: *transfer to Dinard*

Day 6: Thursday 6 July
Stage 5 Dinard to Rennes Individual time-trial 79 km (49 miles)
Stage winner_____
Overall leader_____
Points leader_____
King of the Mountains_____